The Story of Sandy Armistead

A Black Man's Journey in a White Man's World

The Story of Sandy Armistead

A Black Man's Journey in a White Man's World

As Told To
Dwight Norris

The Story of Sandy Armistead:
A Black Man's Journey in a White Man's World
© 2018
Dwight Norris

The photographs in this book are not meant to represent Sandy Armistead or any member of his family. They are provided merely as visual aids to the story presented.

ISBN: 978-1791893361

Cover Photograph by Dwight Norris
Cover Design by Jenny Margotta
Edited by Jenny Margotta
    editorjennymargotta@mail.com or
    www.storiestotellonline/about us

Printed in the United States

Acknowledgments

First of all, my thanks to Sandy Armistead for allowing me to write
his very interesting life story.
My thanks, also, to:
Bob Isbill for contributing a number of great ideas;
Jenny Margotta for her expert editing and support;
and
the High Desert Branch of the California Writers Club critique
group members—Michael Raff, Lorelei Kay, Jeanne Newcomer,
Jerry Lentz, Freddi Gold and Richard Zone—for all their patience
and attention to detail

Prologue

I walked into one of my favorite lunch places—an El Pollo Loco in Apple Valley, California. The time was about 1:30 and I stepped to the back of a long line. Next to me was a black man maybe seventy years old. I thought at this time in the afternoon I might have missed the crowd.

"No matter what time you get here," I said. "You just can't avoid a line."

"Do you know why?" he asked.

"Yeah, I sure do. The food's so good!"

He smiled in agreement.

At the soda machine we both filled our cups.

"So what's *your* story?" I asked, surprising myself.

"What do you mean?"

"Well, you look like you've got a story to tell."

Two and a half hours later I was just beginning to get the picture. The first thing he told me was that he was ninety-seven years old. I dropped my chicken when he said that but quickly recovered. As the time flew by, I realized this man had lived and learned some life lessons that men and women of all races and colors needed to understand.

So here you have it. A white man writing the story of a black man, in this black man's voice, grateful that he's willing to share, and fortunate that he paid attention to what life had to teach. And that he lived long enough to discern it. It's an old story, a simple story that America hasn't heard in a long time.

Chapter 1

My World

My legal name is Herman Edward Armistead. People call me Sandy. My birth date was a long time ago, October 10, 1921. Right now, I am a ninety-seven-year-old man, a happy and proud black man. My daddy always reminded me what happened in that year of my birth, just a few months before I was born. And he told me to never forget it.

On Memorial Day, May 30, 1921, in Tulsa, Oklahoma, a nineteen-year-old Negro shoeshine boy got involved in a skirmish with a seventeen-year old white girl. She was an elevator operator in the Drexel Building at 319 S. Main Street. He was headed to the top floor to a bathroom, the only one in the building he was allowed to use.

Around 4:00 PM, a clerk heard a scream and saw the young black man rush from the building. The elevator operator had cried out, but no one really knew what happened. The police were called and the young man was taken into custody on the morning of Tuesday, May 31st.

Sheriffs questioned the girl, but she didn't want to press charges. Attorneys and other businessmen who worked at the Drexel Building vouched for the boy, stating that he didn't have it in him to assault that girl. But word got out, and blacks gathered at the Tulsa City jail. They knew the nineteen-year-old boy, just by having a conflict with the girl, had done more than enough to get lynched.

The young man was moved to a more secure jail at the top of the Tulsa County Courthouse. Armed white men gathered throughout the evening in the open area around the building. The black men who were on site returned to their homes to pick up rifles and pistols. White men tried to get the sheriff to give the boy up, but the lawman turned them away.

Tensions were mounting, as were the number of armed men surrounding the courthouse—blacks *and* whites. Hundreds of rabble-rousers—some on horseback—now stood around in mobs. A gunshot tore through the hot-blooded night, perhaps fired by a nervous trigger finger, but it led to a full-blown assault. At the end, ten white men lay dead and two blacks.

Men tried to break into National Guard armories but were stopped. Some returned to their homes for arms and ammunition. Around eleven o'clock, unsuspecting patrons from a local theater were let out onto the street, only to walk into thunderous gunfire. The desperation led to the looting of gun shops. This resulted in shattered windows, fires, and the pouring of rioters into the Greenwood district, the most prosperous black community in the country at the time.

Well, I'll spare you any more details, but the bottom line is that in about twenty-four hours, by the night of June 1st, whites had rampaged through Greenwood, and the Red Cross said about three hundred people died, blacks *and* whites. Not only was there shooting, but planes dropping sticks of dynamite. It was an all-out war. In the end, in addition to the dead, over eight hundred were hospitalized. The boy was saved. They didn't lynch him, but I doubt he was ever gonna be the same again. Can you imagine the fear that must have grabbed him by the throat? This whole blow-up became known as the Tulsa Race Riot of 1921. Welcome to my world.

As I say, about three months later, my mother gave birth to me on the kitchen table in the Bronx, New York. I was lucky to be raised by a loving mother and father. I give them the credit for me being the man I am today and for the wonderful life I have lived. There were eight of us children in the family, four brothers and four sisters. We lived through some hard times but never missed a meal. Mama was a full-time wife and mother and had her hands full, raising all of us kids. She kept a clean house and took in laundry and ironing to help pay for all that we needed. She worked hard to give us a home where we had plenty to eat and knew we were loved.

Daddy was a machinist and had the good fortune to work for the Ford Motor Company. Henry Ford built cars even through the Great Depression. We never went without. My father provided the living that put a roof over our heads and filled our home with discipline and peace. He never hit us out of anger, beat us, or slapped us around. I can't remember him ever raising his voice. He was a meek and gentle man and led by example and the wisdom of his ways.

Mama, Daddy, and us eight kids lived in this big, nine-story building at 169th Street and Boston Rd. It was cut up into different apartments. We lived on the fifth floor, and there were three or four apartments on each level. They were called *railroad* apartments, with an aisle down the center and three bedrooms scattered around at one end.

We used to live by kerosene lamps, but this new building had electricity, coal burning stoves, running water, and a big boiler in the basement to heat the radiators. In the winter the superintendent would turn the heat on at six in the morning and turn it off at ten at night. We had all the modern conveniences of the day.

Daddy told us he paid $11.75 a month in rent. This was in the mid- to late '20s. One day the landlord told Daddy he was going to raise the rent by twenty-five cents—make it an even $12.00 a month. Daddy told him he wouldn't pay it. He'd rather move first, so the landlord kept the rent where it was.

Daddy would get up at four in the morning to warm up the stove so Mama could fix us a good breakfast—oatmeal, toast, eggs, and milk. Sometimes even some bacon.

When I wasn't in school, I would help Mama with the laundry. When I was younger we'd heat up the water on the stove and pour it into our corrugated steel tub and put the washboard in it. Then we just had to add some *White King*, and that's where I would do a lot of the washing. Rub and scrub and watch the water turn black. Then throw out the dirty water and get some that was fresh.

After a few years we got the running water that was heated by the boiler in the basement, and we just turned on the faucets.

Mama took in ironing and was really good at making old, wrinkled clothes look brand new. Rich people who couldn't iron so good or didn't want to take the time would pay Mama money, and they seemed to always be happy about how she made their clothes turn out.

The people in our building shared the clotheslines that were strung up between our building and the next one over. When Mama was planning to do some laundry and hang clothes out on the lines, she'd call out the window to our neighbor on the same floor of the next building, "Elsie, you gonna use the clothes lines today?"

If Miss Elsie said, "No," Mama would get busy with the laundry so we'd have clothes to hang out in a couple of hours. In the winter time the clothes would freeze up and the arms of a shirt would stick out straight as if some wooden scarecrow was living in there. It was a funny sight, but it made more work for Mama, who had to bring them inside and set them by the stove to get them dried out.

For a time the tub that we washed the clothes in was the same tub we took our baths in. With ten of us living in that apartment, and the amount of laundry Mama had to do, you can be sure that tub was almost always being used for something.

When we went to the bathroom, we had to go out into the hallway and down to the door at the end. That's where the toilet was. Every floor had its own toilet. When we went in there, we had to pull the chain hanging from the ceiling and a dingy little lightbulb lit up so we could see what we were doing. When we finished we had to flush the toilet clean. And sometimes, there were people waiting in the hallway, hoping we'd hurry up.

I'll never forget the time a large, gray rat was waiting for me in that little toilet closet. Once the light was on, I could see his beady red eyes staring at me. He was sitting right there on the toilet tank, showing no fear. He was bigger than the biggest cat I'd ever seen. I tried to shoo him away with fast hand movements, but like I said, he was fearless, so I had to share the room with him on that occasion.

Sometimes, even with the door closed, that rat would disappear after sitting right there behind me. Daddy said that rats could flatten their bodies and squeeze through the tightest of spaces, like between the bottom of the wall and the floor itself. I grew up wondering if rats even had bones.

At dinner time Mama had even more to do. Fixing food for ten people was a lot of work, though at the time I pretty much took it for granted. I remember that Mama had two or three of us help her get the food ready, and she would switch that around so that if one night Thelma and Bessie and Lawrence were helping her, the rest of us could be out playing until we got called in. Then the next night, a different three of us were the helpers. That way we all did our share and learned how to work in the kitchen. And I think it helped out Mama quite a bit.

She'd usually make a dinner with meat, potatoes, and vegetables. Sometimes chicken, sometimes pork, sometimes beef, but mostly chicken. She'd boil the potatoes and once in a while mash them. Especially if she had some butter in the icebox. That was my favorite. And then spinach or collard greens fried up in bacon grease, or tomatoes, or cabbage. I didn't care for the vegetables so much, but we had to eat them. Sometimes Mama would cook up some brown soup beans with a ham hock in the big pot. Sometimes, some stew. I loved it when she warmed up some bread on the stove, or cooked up some rolls, or biscuits, or cornbread. We'd usually drink milk with our meals.

One thing though. Mama was always the last to eat. She'd

find some kind of last minute thing to do on the stove or in the pots. Or she was dishing stuff out. She was always working to make sure we had enough, and we always did. But only then would she sit down and eat some of the food she fixed for everybody else.

Our father did something for dinner that, at the time, I just thought was the way all families did things. But as I look back, I realize it was part of my father's plan to create something special for his family.

He would come home from work, clean himself up, and dress for dinner. I mean, he wore a fresh shirt, and a coat and tie, and shined up his fancy shoes. He made us feel like this was a special occasion, a time for us all to be together, and that he loved us more than anybody else in the whole world. And I believe that to be true. And he always offered thanks at each and every meal.

He would ask us about our day and the things we did and what we said to others. Then he would tell us some stories about this little boy or that little girl. These little boys and girls ended up facing the same problems that *we* did. It was amazing! Of course, as I look back I realize that my father was just making up stories to help us see the right way to go and make good choices when he wasn't around.

He told us, "Always do the right thing, even if it's hard to do at the time. Always be honest."

And he said, "Always treat others like you would want to be treated." He called that the *Golden Rule*. I began to understand that my father was always thinking about his family and wanted to do what was best for us. He wanted to teach us to learn the practical lessons of life. He wanted us all to take responsibility for ourselves and be independent. And he wanted us to think for ourselves and not just run with the crowd.

One time when Mama called us to come to dinner, I kept playing. I didn't come in right away. When I finally walked in, my father said, "Why you so late? You heard your Mama call you, didn't you?"

"Yes, I did."

"Well, since you're not that interested in dinner, then you don't get any today." And he made me sit at the table without eating while everyone around me was getting all they wanted. I felt terrible!

That night, after I went to bed, Mama came into the boys' bedroom with a basket of food and brought a cookie for me and each of my brothers. I would have my dinner after all! Oh, it was so good, and I loved Mama so much for doing that.

A few weeks later I was late again. Just got caught up playing hide-n-seek and running around. Daddy sounded much like he did the first time.

The reason I was often late for dinner

"Did you hear your mama call you for dinner?"

"Yes," I said.

"When your mama calls you for dinner, you need to come. No dinner for you tonight."

His words struck me like a punch in the gut. Would Mama rescue me again? Or would I, this time, have to pay the price?

Mama walked around the table, dishing out generous helpings of her yummy mashed potatoes. She wouldn't even look at me, but when she thought my head was down, I caught her giving Daddy a knowing grin and then a wink, and Daddy returned the wink.

That's when I knew! My parents were teaching me and taking care of me at the same time. This seemed pretty good to me—a strict lesson in discipline but a soft place to land in case I hadn't learned it yet. It made me want to try harder to do what they wanted me to do. The fried chicken, mashed potatoes, and other fixings were delicious that night, but I never again failed to follow Mama's instructions to come in. I just couldn't take advantage of Mama and Daddy's goodness.

But I did have one problem which would follow me all my life. I was very curious.

If I saw a hill, I wanted to know what was on the other side. If it was a mountain, I wanted to know what was on top. If it was a locked door, I wanted to know what was behind it. Always wanting to explore and discover.

My father would say, "Don't go in there."

And I would say, "Why not?"

One Saturday my father and I sat on the porch of our apartment building and watched a long line of railroad cars roll by. I must have been about five or six years old, and I counted the cars one after another. I remember counting to one hundred and sixty-two.

"Where are those cars going, Daddy? What's in them? Are they all going to the same place?"

My curiosity would drive lots of adventures in my life and teach me many lessons. And with all of them, my father's voice was right there beside me.

Chapter 2

Independence

For the next few years, time crawled by. I was tired of being six, and then seven, and then eight. Single-digit numbers. I couldn't wait to be ten! Ten was *double* digits, and then I would *be* somebody! Little did I know how many digits I would accumulate in my life as time began to race by.

Just before my tenth birthday, my father thought it was time for him to teach me how to hustle. "I'm gonna loan you a dollar," he said. "I ain't giving you nothing. You're gonna pay me back this dollar."

"Okay," I said, not knowing how I could do that.

Daddy took me down to *The New York Times* building on 43rd Street, where we spent that dollar and bought fifty newspapers—two cents apiece.

"Now, you're gonna take these papers out to a good street corner," he said. "One where lots of people are walking by, and you're gonna sell them."

"How much they sell for, Daddy?"

"Three cents," he said. "And that's how you're gonna pay me back."

So for every dollar I invested, I could make a dollar fifty. But I soon caught on to the idea that whatever newspapers I bought, I needed to sell them the same day. Otherwise, it was like trying to sell a rotten tomato. Nobody was looking to buy yesterday's newspaper. Even this first batch, I had to stay out late to get those papers sold.

In fact, it didn't take me too long to see that if I didn't sell at least thirty-three of those fifty papers, I wouldn't even make my dollar back. In fact, thirty-three at three cents apiece would fall just short of a dollar, at ninety-nine cents. It wasn't until I sold that thirty-fourth paper that I started to make a profit. And then I'd keep the whole three cents on each paper I sold after that, right up to fifty, and that's how I made that fifty cents.

Paid my father back in a week, and then I had money in my pocket. But I had a problem. The street corner where I was selling the papers—229th Street and 5th Avenue—was four blocks from where the newspaper building was. Now, I could get to the newspaper building from home by hitching a ride on the back of a trolley. No problem. But walking down there to the corner, carrying those papers under each arm, was not easy. That was a lot of papers. Sometimes, I'd drop some of them. One time a couple of them blew away, and if they were dirty or torn up, it was harder to sell them. People didn't want messed up papers.

So I took two dollars of what I had earned and bought a kid's old *Red Flyer* wagon. I'd hitch the wagon to my back with a small piece of rope and *still* take a cool ride on the back of that trolley. After I jumped off at 229th Street, I stacked those newspapers on the wagon and stuck a rock on top of the pile, and I got down to that corner faster, and the papers were clean and straight. This worked out real good. Took me less time to sell fifty papers.

But there were some days I couldn't sell all fifty papers. Don't know what it was. Maybe not as many people walking by. Maybe didn't want to spend the money. Maybe in too big of a hurry. Remember, if I don't sell those last sixteen papers, I'm not making my fifty cents.

I got to where I knew this business pretty good. My father believed in teaching me by letting me make my mistakes—find out by doing, not just telling me. If he'd have just told me stuff, I probably wouldn't believe the half of it. This way I knew how it worked firsthand. But he was still there, just the same, to offer suggestions when he saw a problem. My father made sure I saved at least half my money so I'd have it for the future.

"You know, son, you're doing good, and I'm proud of you," my daddy said. "But if you had a paper route, all those people would be committed to buying a paper from you every day of the month. Wouldn't be no ups and downs. You'd just have to deliver the papers."

"How would I do that?"

"*The Times*, they got subscribers. You know, people already signed up. They give you the names and addresses, and you just drop the paper at their door."

"But how would I get the papers *to* their doors? I couldn't do it with the wagon."

"I'll tell you what. Let's find a good used Schwinn. I'll put up half the money and you put up half the money, and you can pay me back."

"Yeah, I know," I said. "How much you think that would cost us?"

"Get me one of your newspapers, and we'll take a look."

Daddy held the newspaper in his lap for a long time, just moaning and groaning without telling me much of anything. He marked up some ads with a pencil and then started talking.

"Well, I know that a new Schwinn sells for about thirty bucks. But we ain't getting a new bike. I see ads here for eight, ten, twelve bucks. But I think we can do better than that."

"What should we do?"

"To get the best buy, we need to be talking to somebody who don't want or need the bike anymore, for whatever reason. Maybe it belonged to somebody else, but now it belongs to them and they ain't gonna use it. Don't need it."

"And how do we find that out?" I asked.

"Well, they ain't gonna put that in the ad. We just gotta talk to the people a little bit."

"We gonna walk?"

"Yes. These addresses are within walking distance."

"Okay, let's go," I said.

"One more thing," Daddy said. "If we gonna negotiate a good buy, we got to have the cash with us. Nothing worse than getting people to agree to a good price and not being able to give them the money."

"What should we bring?" I asked.

"You got some cash and you got some coins?" Daddy asked. "Bring me three one-dollar bills and four quarters." With that, we were on our way. The first house we stopped at was two blocks down and three blocks over. Asking price was sixteen bucks.

"Is that the best you can do on the price?" Daddy asked.

"Yes, it is," the man said. "If you looking to steal this bike, then just get on out of here!" And he slammed the door.

Next house was a little farther south. Bike already gone.

The third and last house brought us four blocks back up in the other direction, closer to the city. Daddy knocked on the door, and a middle-aged woman answered.

"Hi," Daddy said. "We're here about the bike. Do you still have it?"

"Yes. Meet me around the side of the house."

When we got there, the lady was standing with the bike. It was four years old, red, and barely a scratch on it. Tires looked good too.

"How much are you asking for the bike?" Daddy asked.

"Ten dollars," she answered.

"Is that the best you can do on the price?"

"Well, I could come down a little bit maybe."

"Why are you selling it?"

"Oh, my father used to ride it for exercise. He lived up in Rockville Center. Passed away last month. Just trying to get rid of his stuff."

"How about five dollars?" Daddy asked. "We'll take good care of it and put it to good use."

"Five dollars?" she said. "That don't sound like very much. It's a *Schwinn*, you know."

"Yes, Ma'am, it looks like a fine bike. My son needs it for a paper route to earn some money."

The woman stood still and stared at Daddy.

"I'll tell you what," Daddy said. "We'll make it six dollars, and we can give you cash right now. What do you say?"

He held our six one-dollar bills in his outstretched hand. The woman reached for it and thanked him. When Daddy and I talked about this deal later, he explained that we never would have gotten this price on the first bike where the seller was asking sixteen dollars. He was not flexible, and it would have been a waste of our time to try to talk him into it. Can't fit a square peg into a round hole. Got to put yourself in front of the right people.

The second bike was gone, which shows the bike was something people wanted. But the third stop had the features we needed. She had never used the bike, was never going to use it, and didn't seem like she wanted it around. It took up space and maybe reminded her of her father, who passed away. So this deal had flexibility built into it.

Daddy helped me put a large basket on the front of the bike to hold the papers. I got a route of seventy-five customers. I could only hold half the papers at a time. I started making about twenty-two dollars a month before tips, including dailies and Sundays. All after school and on weekends. Not bad for a kid. Could have helped Daddy pay that twenty-five cent rent increase, no sweat. But he wouldn't have taken it.

In a couple of years, I bought myself a brand new Schwinn, red and shiny. No scratches at all. It was a 1933 Aerocycle with balloon, white-wall tires. Caused quite a stir when I rode it downtown. So I'm about twelve years old and doing all right for myself. I *knew* I'd be somebody after I hit double digits.

In those days I learned that making money wasn't all that hard. All you had to do was figure out what people wanted or needed and work out a way to give it to them. I was proving that with the newspapers.

But if you hang out around Grand Central Station on 42nd

Street, or around a subway station, another opportunity presents itself. Lots of men were dressed for business and heading for a meeting. What they wanted was to look good, and lots of them hoped they could get their shoes shined before they showed up.

Competition right down the street

So, for a couple of years, I had my paper route along with a shoeshine stand. To shine shoes I didn't need no fancy chair or nothing. My customers would just lean up against the building and put their foot up on the box that I carried.

And I'd make their shoes look real good.

Then there would be those windy days in the city where men were walking to the subway or the trolley. They were all dressed up for a business meeting, and a gust of wind would take their fedora or their homburg right off their heads, so it's blowing down the street like a tumbleweed in the desert. When one of us kids would snag the hat for them, they were more than happy to reward us with a shiny new coin, whatever they could grab out of their pocket.

Money was everywhere. But as good as things were, I was soon to be offered an even greater opportunity to make some really big money.

Chapter 3

The Gangs of New York

I'm about fourteen now, and I'm doing all right. I still got my 1933 Schwinn Aerocycle, and I'm riding it all over the city. I'm taking lessons from the big boys, the Mob and the Brothers. They run numbers, and they decided to split their territory, with the Mob taking the north side of Manhattan and the Brothers taking the south side.

Now, I'm not running numbers, but I got my territories. I shine shoes and sell my newspapers. I guess I didn't go unnoticed, because one day I'm at one of my shoeshine locations. Suddenly, I'm surrounded by three guys, and my Schwinn is tearing down the street, ridden by one of their friends. I turn to run after my bike, but the three guys grab me. They walk me around the corner into an alleyway.

The leader of the gang was a guy named Adolfo. I remember *his* name; the others I forget. A skinny guy with a moustache carried a little satchel. "I am the leader of the *Gauchos,* a Puerto Rican gang," Adolfo told me. "You got a problem with that?"

"No," I said. "I got a problem that you stole my bike."

"We will give the bike back," he said. "If you do what we tell you."

Adolfo and his friends explained they wanted me to steal a car.

"Why would I want to do that?" I asked.

"For one thing," Adolfo said. "You do that, you get your bike back.

"And for another thing, we won't beat you up," the kid in the green shirt said. "You stay healthy."

I can't believe I'm hearing these words. They're threatening to kick my ass. We're just on the edge of the alley and I can see people walking by. Some of them are looking our way, but nobody's saying anything or doing anything. Everybody's in a hurry.

The gangs of New York

"And besides that, once you get good at this, you can make some real money," Adolfo said.

"I make money," I said. "I got my own business."

They laughed.

"You make peanuts," the round-faced fat guy said. "When you working for us, you be making fifteen, twenty bucks a pop, just like that."

"Your mama ain't gonna give you that kind of money."

That kind of money sounded good. I knew I'd be taking a risk, and I didn't mind that so much. But I knew I'd be doing wrong. Daddy sure taught us the difference between right and wrong. But Daddy was a goody two-shoes. Never drove a car, never cussed, never even raised his voice. I liked that in my dad 'cause it gave me less to worry about, but I never felt like I had to be that way. Deep down, I guess I didn't feel like a goody two-shoes. I didn't mind bending the rules a little bit, long as nobody got hurt.

"But I'm only fourteen. I don't know how to drive, and I don't know how to steal a car."

Adolfo smiled and put his arm over my shoulders. "We fix you right up," he said.

We walked for quite a while, blocks up and over, part of the city where there's less foot traffic, but there were still cars parked on the street, kind of like an industrial area. We go up to this car and Adolfo gets into the satchel. Pulls out a shim—a flat piece of steel—shoves it down alongside the window by the driver's seat and pops open the lock. Door opens just like that.

We jump into the car. A couple of the guys stay outside on the street, watching. Now, Adolfo reaches under the steering column near where the ignition is and yanks out some wires. He strips the ends of the wires with a pocket knife and touches the bare ends together, and *vroom*, the engine's up and running.

Soon as the others hear the engine, they jump into the back seat and off we go. Adolfo's driving, but he's trying to show me how to work the clutch and the shift. Now, he's trying to go fast to get away, but he's also looking down and looking at me, and he doesn't see this car coming, and *kablaam!* We hit pretty hard, and there we are in the middle of this big intersection, and all these guys split and start scattering like cockroaches when the lights come on.

I'm the last one to hit the streets, but the first one to get grabbed by the collar. This cop puts me in handcuffs and shoves me into the back of his car. Things are moving so fast, and all of a sudden everything's stopped. After a long time in the back of that car, they drive me down to the police station and put me in a jail cell. I had to tell them who I was and where I lived, and they went down and picked up my mama and daddy.

Lord, have mercy! Mama was yelling and trying to get at me. She was the spicy one. Daddy was just standing back there, looking all serious, like he was sad and disappointed. After some papers were signed, this one cop said he would drive us home. I sat in the back seat with Mama, and Daddy sat in the front with the cop. Mama was screaming all the way home. I felt safer in the jail cell.

After the cop dropped us off, Daddy took me into their bedroom and sat me down. "Did you do what the police say you did?" Daddy asked. "Did you help steal that car?"

"Yes, I did that."

"Do you know why you did that?"

"They were gonna beat me up if I didn't go with them," I said. "And I guess I felt cool to be with them. They thought *I* was cool."

"Did you feel cool all the way to the jail?" Daddy asked. "Did you feel cool when you looked into your mama's eyes?"

I remember just hanging my head and tears started pouring down my cheeks.

My daddy put his hand on my arm and pulled me toward him. "Because you were honest, I'm not gonna spank you, but if this happens again ..."

Just then Mama walked in. "The police officer came back and wants to talk to Sandy."

We all sat at the kitchen table: Officer O'Reilly, Mama, Daddy, and me. My brothers and sisters were told to go to their bedrooms.

"Sandy, this is the first time the police department has heard about you," the officer said. "You ever try to steal a car before?"

"No, sir."

"And you never spent any time in the jail before?"

"No, sir."

"Your parents tell me you're a good boy. You got a paper route, you shine shoes, you go to school."

"Yes, sir."

"Do you respect your parents?"

"Yes, sir. I *love* my parents."

I noticed right then that tears were rolling down Daddy's cheek and Mama's face was all sunk into itself, like she couldn't bring herself to say what she was really feeling.

"From everything I can see," Officer O'Reilly continued. "You got a good family and you've been doing the right things, going to school, and making your own money in an honest way. What made you go with these guys to steal that car?"

"Well, they stole my bike and said I'd get it back if I went with them. And they said they'd beat me up if I didn't go."

"Let me tell you something," the officer said. "You hang around with them, they *will* beat you up to keep you in line. If you got nothing to do with them, they forget about you and move on to other guys and threaten *them*. You're better off without them.

"If you steal cars, you *will* get caught. There's no way for you *not* to get caught. And you *will* go to jail. And if you keep doing it, you start stealing from stores and you're carrying a gun, and you break into people's houses and steal from them, and then you go to jail for longer and longer times, and you'll be kept away from your friends and your family.

"And you'll be around scumbags who live like gutter rats, who will not be nice to you but will find a way to get something out of you, and they *will* hurt you. They don't give a shit about you, no matter what they tell you at the beginning.

"Looks like you got a nice family and a nice life going on without these punks. I hope you decide not to go down their path in life."

I listened to what Officer O'Reilly had to say, and as time went on, I realized he was right. I noticed some kids in the neighborhood hanging around with the gangsters, and they would disappear for a while, and I wondered what happened to them, if they were in jail or something.

My grandfather was a slave, and he had to do what his

master told him. I figured if I became a gang member, all them other guys would be my masters and I would be their slave. I would have to do what they told me. I was full of piss and vinegar, but I wasn't stupid. I didn't want to be a slave like my grandfather, only in a different way. That would be a bad thing.

That cop set me straight. He cared enough to take the time to come and sit down with me and my parents and lay it out for us. And he was a white man. Wasn't a lot of black cops back in the day, because, when you had a confrontation out there on the streets, only one person could be in charge, and that had to be the cop. Back then lots of white men didn't want to submit to the authority of a black man, even in New York, and even if he was wearing a badge. And in the South it was unheard of that a black man could be a cop.

When I think back about it, it was always the white man who helped me. The black man was too bitter to help. He was all into his own needs and, generally, so needy because he was mostly aware of what he didn't have. All he could see was what he was missing. He had nothing to give. He could have had something to give but could never put his hands on it because his mind was somewhere else.

The white man had something to offer because he had the resources. He could offer you a job or some advice about the best way to go. And there are plenty of white men who will help you if you treat them with respect and like you are a decent person as well. You treat them like you're some kind of thug looking to hurt them, they just want to get away from you. You do that, you just created fear, and they don't want to get hurt. Don't know anybody who does. But respect goes two ways, and sometimes it's gotta start with you.

I have friends who say to me, "Sandy, how can you not hate the blue-eyed devil?" I will be the first to admit that back in the day the black man endured a lot of bad shit. *Really* bad shit. But we've come a long ways since then, my brothers. It's not like it used to be. We defeat ourselves if we look at the worst of times and deny the opportunities available to us now. And I can't think of the last time hatred got me anywhere.

So I was grateful to Officer O'Reilly, who cared enough to set me straight. And when I see a cop today, I tell him how a long time ago one of his friends in the police brotherhood cared enough to straighten me out, and I thank him for it.

I never stood face to face with Adolfo and his gang again. I saw them a time or two, but they were running another kid around, just like Officer O'Reilly said.

And, thanks to the police department I finally got my bike back, but it was never the same. And neither was I.

Chapter 4

Slavery

I want to say more about my grandfather being a slave. My ancestors had African names, but we bore the family name *Armistead* because my grandfather was the *property* of Lewis Armistead, a Confederate General who was mortally wounded on Cemetery Ridge in the Battle of Gettysburg. He died two days later in a Union field hospital at the age of forty-six.

You can read about Lewis Armistead. He was regarded as a fine man. He was good friends with General Winfield Scott Hancock, a Union general. They had been friends for seventeen years. General Hancock was wounded in the same battle as General Armistead, but he pulled through. It must have been hard for those two good men to be on opposite sides in a battle to the death. And it must have been even harder for my grandfather to be a slave.

The idea of a man being owned by another man has always been foreign to my way of thinking. I cannot relate to it. I know that throughout time slavery has existed all over the world, for thousands of years, probably every culture. All kinds of people owning slaves. Even blacks selling blacks and whites selling whites.

Slavery was a bad deal all around. The idea that one man could own another, a worker that he controlled, could force him to work 'til he couldn't work no more, could beat him and chain him, and not pay him nothing for his labor. Stole his freedom and his dignity to where he felt worthless as a whipped dog. No way for anyone to live. Steal the joy right out of a man's soul.

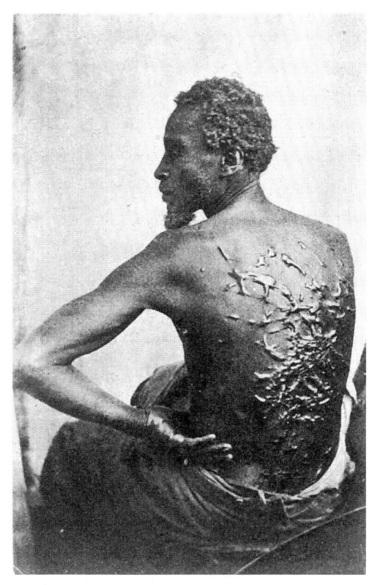

Never the same again

How could any man bear up under it? He had to work all day long to please his master. "Yes, Massa, Yes, Massa," all throughout the long hot hours of the day. Under the blazing hot sun working in the tobacco fields, or picking cotton and bleeding from the fingertips, not able to eat or drink some cool water when he wanted to. Don't see how anyone could do that. But even worse, if that worker had a family—a wife and a child—the owner could come in anytime he wanted and beat the child or rape the man's wife. After all, these weren't people. They were *property*. Lord have mercy! What kind of living is that? Who would want to wake up the next morning with a life like that? How could any man, woman, or child be happy?

And even the slave owner, how could this kind of a life be good for him? Where is his self-respect? How could he live with himself? How could he look in the mirror, knowing he brought such brutality and despair and pain into the lives of so many? How can he accept the forced labor of men and women whose efforts cost him nothing? Wouldn't such a man get fat, and lazy, and thankless, and blinded to his faults? This system of slavery was no good for anyone involved in it, not even the slave master. Must have been all about the money.

To my way of thinking, the character of the *master* did not measure up to the character of most slaves. At least they were hard workers. The slave masters took from the slave what they didn't have the right to take. They were undeserving and selfish. Many of them cruel, so cruel. And nothing could touch them. They were drunk on the money.

I heard that some slave masters were kind, even friendly with their slaves, treated them more like people, even family, but still, the slaves had no freedom to make decisions for themselves. No right to get an education, own their own land, move their families out on their own and be independent. No way to live. No way to live. Just not right.

I never knew my grandfather—he died before I was born. I don't know *when* he died—if while in slavery or after emancipation. If he died after emancipation, don't know where he went after being set free. Most slaves didn't know what to do or where to go at that point. Many stayed with the farm and the family that owned them, but now as a freedman, earning some kind of wages for their work. I believe my father knew a lot about his father's slavery, but it set kind of heavy on his shoulders, and I never heard him talk about it. He didn't believe in placing such a load on the heart of a child.

A terrible existence

But I had a natural curiosity about my *own* heritage, so I did some reading. I decided to start with Lewis Armistead since there was no way to read about my grandfather. I didn't even know his name.

But Lewis Armistead was easy to find in the history books. He was of English descent, and since the early 1600s his family had occupied the area that became the state of Virginia. Don't know what they did in the Revolutionary War, but they must have done something in fighting for independence. I know Armistead had five uncles who fought in the War of 1812, and one of them, Major George Armistead, was the commander of Ft. McHenry in Baltimore, defending Baltimore Harbor. This is when Francis Scott Key wrote the words that would become our National Anthem, the "Star Spangled Banner," the song that honors our flag, the one that some people won't stand up for anymore.

Now, the fact that Lewis Armistead was the *owner* or *slave master* of my grandfather doesn't give him a special place in my heart, except as he was connected to my grandfather and that that fact could maybe shed some light on my grandfather's life. So here's what I'm putting together. The Armisteads lived in Virginia, and my father was born in Petersburg, Virginia. So I'm thinking that my grandfather lived his life as a slave in Virginia.

Now, I didn't want to limit my research to the Armistead family. I also wanted to read some general history. I was born in 1921, and I don't know my father's exact birthday, but I figure he must have been somewhere between twenty and forty years of age when he became my father. That would have put his birthday somewhere between 1881 and 1901, would be my guess.

If you back up the dates for my grandfather's age in a similar way, he could likely have been born between 1841 and 1861, obviously before the Civil War, but also in a prime age where they would want him for his strength and abilities as a laborer while slavery was still being practiced. If he was born around 1840, he would have been twenty-five years of age when the Civil War ended.

These dates are good for me to think about for another important reason. In 1807 the United States made it illegal to import slaves from outside the country, and that law took effect in January of 1808. So it makes it very unlikely, to my way of thinking, that my grandfather could have been born before 1808 in Africa and transported on a slave ship to this country. I find some comfort in that. I believe he was born into a slave family in Virginia, grew up with his mother and father and brothers and sisters on a plantation, and had an upbringing where he was loved and treated well. It's possible, and that's what I choose to believe, based on the facts as I know them. And that's what I *do believe.* By saying this I am not making any excuses for slavery. The horrors of it have never been understood by those who haven't been touched by it.

Coffled together

The journey from Africa to the United States was rough. I've done some reading on this, too. People who had been kidnapped to be slaves in this country were regarded as property, and the slave traders were paid only after delivering a live slave and exchanging him or her for cash. So the slave trader was as brutal as he needed to be to get them here without killing them. They didn't bind them individually lest one of the captives make a break for it, whether on land or water. They manacled them together—*coffling* they called it.

Heavy chains were looped around one's neck and draped over the shoulder and around the neck of the next man as well. Five or more could be connected like this. Sometimes, ankles and wrists were bound in the same way. There was no way to escape from such coffling, and if one did, they were subject to beatings and lashings and brutality that would nearly kill them and strike fear in the hearts of the remaining captives.

When slave ships landed on the east coast of the United States, the prisoners had to be transported usually hundreds of miles to the slave market. The Good Book says that mankind was created in the image of God. Yet at the end of this journey, individuals were placed on the block to be sold like a slab of beef. What was their transportation? Most had to walk—manacled, coffled, and barefoot. Their feet bled, but they had to keep pace or get whipped. Their drivers rode horses and wagons and cracked the lash.

The journey was filled with violence to keep the captives from escaping. Beatings, stabbings, rapes—whatever it took to keep the prisoners in line. On the trading block, men were sold into servitude for the labor they could provide, either in the cotton fields, tobacco plantations, or blacksmith shop. It was not unusual for the women to be sold directly into sexual servitude, to bear children and be a sex slave for their master.

When a slave owner needed cash, he would do what some do today. He would sell a piece of property to get what he needed. Since families of slaves were just thought of as property, it was not uncommon to divide a slave family by selling off a brother or sister just because their owner needed cash. Nobody listened to cries for mercy. The cruelty was indescribable.

A child's grief as a slave

Let me tell you that people who were enslaved like this were far more than what their captors thought they were. They were people with love in their hearts and intelligence and creativity in their minds. Their hopes and dreams were driven far from them, but if given the chance, who can imagine the lives and families they would have created? I'll bet my grandfather would have even taught me how to fish.

Though I don't believe that my grandfather was brought to the States over the seas, I have often wondered if he wore an iron collar around his neck, forged in the blacksmith's shop, or an iron bracelet around his wrist that labeled him, *Property of Lewis Armistead.*

I have now lived more than twice the number of years as my grandfather's captor, and there is nothing that would make me envy his lifestyle. And though I fall short of the glory of God every day of my life, I am thankful that I have not laid the sin of *slave master* upon my soul.

No way to escape

Chapter 5

My Life as a Hobo

I'm fifteen years old now. I keep delivering papers, and shining shoes, and going to school, but I'm getting restless.

At the end of every month, when I collected for my paper route, I'd pile the coins on my bed in a big mound, and it looked like so much money. I kept saving much of it like Daddy said.

I wanted to take that money and hit the road. I wanted to explore. I couldn't sit at home my whole life. I had to get out there and see what's going on in other places. See what people are like all over the country. So this one evening after supper I sat down with Mama and Daddy at the kitchen table and told them I gotta go.

"What you mean you gotta go?" Mama asked.

"I gotta leave home," I said. "You know, get out there like a hobo."

"Like a hobo!" Mama screamed. Then she started running around the kitchen like she was chasing two rats at the same time going in different directions. Then she screamed some more. Daddy got up and wrapped his arms around her.

"Let him go," he said. "Make a man out of him."

I took a day to get ready to leave. Packed a knapsack with some extra clothes. Mama fixed me enough food for a week and fresh laundry to last about five days. Lord have mercy!

"Mama, how am I gonna carry all that?" I asked. "I'm a hobo, not a paying customer on a passenger car where the porters are gonna help you out."

I brought a hundred dollars with me, just in case. I knew

there was a risk of it being lost or stolen, so I put half of it in my pocket, and half of it in my knapsack.

Mama put her arms around me and cried one more time. Daddy hugged me and shed a tear or two. I took enough food for one day and whatever would fit in the knapsack. That first day I hitched a ride down to Grand Central Station and hopped on a passenger train. I know I said I wasn't gonna be traveling that way, but I wanted to get out of the New York area quickly, you know, get a change of scenery and begin my new life. I actually rode overnight on a Pullman to Portland, Maine, and ate breakfast. From there I'd look for a freight train and head west.

I walked to the outskirts of the train station, and I could see the freight-train storage yard. I strutted down the track and around a fence that separated the passenger trains from the freights. I walked past boxcars, flatcars, engines that had not yet been hooked up to a string of cars, and other cars I didn't even know the names of.

It's one thing to see freight cars being pulled along the track from a distance. Almost look like toys. But it's a whole other thing to be standing right there next to one. Put your hand on it and feel the hard steel. Dwarfs you like an ant next to a Model-T. Must weigh tons. I knew right away, if I was ever gonna see Mama and Daddy alive again, I had to respect these freight cars.

I kept walking and pretty soon I smelled what seemed like coffee. Could it be? Ahead to my right, at the bottom of the slope leading up to the track, flickered a little campfire, with a coffee pot and some tin cans, surrounded by about six hobos.

As I got close one of the men stood up and came over to welcome me. I'd say he was about Daddy's age and tall, with a scruffy beard. It was summertime so nobody was wearing any coats. The tall man was named Carl. He introduced me around. I still remember his name to this day because he helped me out a lot—maybe even saved my life. One of the men handed me a cup of coffee.

"So, where you headed, young man?"

"Well, just exploring. Heading down the track wherever the train will take me."

"You ever done this before?" one of the others asked.

"Nope," I said. "Just starting out."

"What kind of supplies you got?" Carl asked.

"Oh, I got a lot of stuff," I answered. "Right here in my knapsack."

"Mind if I take a look?" Carl asked.

I was mostly comfortable letting him look in my knapsack. He could have taken the whole thing anyway if he wanted to. But it seemed to me like I could trust him, even though half my money was right there in the coin purse. I was starting to get the idea out on the rail that you had to trust somebody. Maybe that's why these guys were traveling together.

Carl started taking stuff out of my knapsack. Once he got the clothes out, there wasn't much left to look at.

"What are you gonna wear for shoes?" he asked.

"Already got them on," I said. "These sneakers."

Carl gave me a funny look, and some of the other guys snickered. "Do you have an empty milk bottle?" Carl asked.

"No."

"Do you have anything to store some water in?"

"No."

"You got a handkerchief?"

"No. What do I need all that stuff for?"

"These sneakers you're wearing aren't gonna last you a week if you're hopping freights," Carl said. "And you need an empty milk bottle 'cause you gotta piss in something, unless you just want to spray everybody in an open box car. And you need another empty milk bottle so you can store some water. And you need a handkerchief in case the freight you're riding gets stopped in a long tunnel. You got to breathe through a wet handkerchief. And there's some other things you're gonna need. There's a General Store just down the road. You got some money with you?"

"Oh boy," I thought. "There goes the money."

While I was hesitating about answering the question, Carl saw the coin purse in my knapsack and snatched it.

"This where you're keeping your money?" he asked, holding it up.

A short, fat guy, whose name I had already forgotten, said, "Don't worry. Nobody's gonna steal your money. And just to be sure, take out what you need for a pair of construction boots and a couple of bottles of milk, and I'll hold the rest of it 'til you get back."

"My ass!" yelled Carl.

So Carl took me under his wing and escorted me to the General Store. In addition to what he already told me about, I ended up buying a good blanket. It might be summertime right now, but that didn't mean it would be warm 'round the clock. I also bought a waterproof rain coat. Carl said the weather could change suddenly in the course of a day. On a freight train crossing the country, a man had to protect himself from sudden temperature changes and the weather. He also got the store to give me an empty cardboard box for insulation and to ease up on the strong rail car vibration.

When we got back to the rail yard, we found the men at the campfire had broken camp and scattered the ashes so you could barely tell where the fire had been.

"Keeps the bulls happy," Carl explained.

"The bulls?"

"The bulls are the railroad cops. In a rail yard, they're always nearby. Their job is to protect the railroad property and to run you off. They carry these big sticks, like police batons, and they swing them at you. If they whack you across the back, or on the arm or leg, you're in a world of hurt. If they hit you in the head, God help you. But they usually keep it on a friendly basis."

While we were gone, a long freight train had pulled up on the track. Lots of cars.

"Where's your friends?" I asked. "On this train?"

"Well, they could be," Carl said. "Or they could have climbed to the other side of it. There's another freight train sitting right over there."

"How do you know that?"

"I saw it as we walked up," Carl said. "If you're gonna survive out here, you gotta notice what's going on around you, close by and far down the track."

"Makes sense," I said.

"Now, if you wanted to get to the other side of this train, what do you think would be the best way to do it?" Carl asked.

I knelt down and looked to the underside of the train. "Scooting through here would probably be the quickest," I said.

"Yeah, quickest way to get yourself killed," Carl said. "And you don't cross between the cars either, where the coupling is. These cars could shift five feet with no warning at all. Throw you right down there on the tracks and run you over."

Later, as I thought about it, I was glad for what Carl taught me. I should have already known a lot of this because of my own experience. I had ridden on lots of buses and trolleys, more often than not hanging on from the outside somehow. I knew about their jerky motions, the sudden starts and stops that throw you off balance. On a trolley I would always keep my hands and feet grounded on handles or grips or hand-holds. To climb or move around, I would move only one limb at a time. The freight train is so much larger and heavier; it's hard to imagine how much more powerful it is. You might have only one chance to learn that lesson, and it would be too late.

That day in the freight yard, Carl taught me the safest way to jump on a moving train. The best way, of course, is to jump on a train that's not moving yet, but it makes you more likely to run into a bull, and it also gives you the possibility of sitting on that train for a long time. It might not even be hooked up to an engine.

But this freight was headed west, and that's what we all wanted. We were ducking bulls and didn't want to sit in a stifling freight car for hours, so as this BNSF started to move, so did we.

Carl taught me that a successful mounting on a moving boxcar involved a lot of things—your height and weight, your speed, the firmness and slope of the gravel that led up to the track, and the speed the train was moving. He said if you can't count the bolts in the center of the wheel, don't try to get on that train. If it's a blur, that train is moving too fast.

You had to throw your bag on first, and as you're running up, hopefully, you're gaining on a steel foothold that looks like the bottom of a ladder. Turns out a lot of men made the leap and tried to land on that first step with their foot. They slipped through and were left hanging upside down by a leg as the train picks up speed, or they fell out, only to be chewed up by the speedy spinning wheels that are stalking from behind.

Carl told me not to aim with my foot, but to throw my bent knee into the space above that first step. It's a more sturdy hold and will not allow me to slip and fall through. Then with a solid base, I can use my arms to jockey myself onto the bed of the freight car. Who knows how many times Carl may have saved my life?

I rode the rails with Carl and his band of hobos all the way to the West Coast and into the winter months. The scenery was beautiful, no doubt about it. The waving corn fields of Iowa, the mountain peaks and tunnels of Colorado, the tall trestles that carried the trains over steep canyons. Giant elk on the northern plains of North Dakota and Montana, and the tall, thick trees of Washington.

We celebrated my sixteenth birthday with a campfire along the tracks in Snohomish, Washington. Reminded me of the fire they had back in Maine when I first walked into their camp. Even blew out the candles on a birthday cake the boys chipped in for from a local bakery.

Winter was close, and we decided to hop a freight back East so we could see the land with a blanket of snow. We dropped down south to Oregon. It was now mid-November with a chill in the air, and our eastbound journey would carry us through the widest part of Idaho, as well as Wyoming, South Dakota, and Minnesota. I knew what snow was like in New York, but this journey gave new meaning to the word *cold*.

As much as I appreciated what I learned from Carl and his friends, and the sights that I had seen—the wildlife and scenery—I was getting restless again. I wanted to keep moving, but I wanted to meet people and get to know about them and how they lived. Carl and his group were the first ones I met, but I was ready to meet some more. Before I got home I wanted to visit California. I needed some sunshine and a little more warmth. I wanted to see what the State was about, and what the people were like.

I knew I had made some good friends, but we parted ways in upstate New York. No shortage of snow there either. We all had some money on us from odd jobs we had done along the way. After all, we weren't bums, just hobos. Because of the hardships of the last couple of weeks, we ate dinner at a nice restaurant and got rooms at a hotel on the corner. The hot bath felt wonderful. We said our goodbyes in the morning.

I hopped a freight that was headed west.

California was hard to believe—seventy degrees in the wintertime, beautiful beaches, seagulls flying overhead, girls in bikinis. Are you kidding me? I could get used to this.

It was common in those days—the 1930s—for towns and cities to offer vouchers for travelers. We'd get one week free room and board. This was true in many places all over the country. I suppose it had to do with the fact that we were fighting our way out of the Great Depression, and it was one way people could help out.

People were warm and caring in those days. I remember one time walking down the road, and this young lady, a white lady, passed me in her car. She stopped and backed up and called out, "Have you had lunch yet?"

"Can you see me?" I said. "I'm black."

"Yes, I can see you."

She invited me to ride in her car to the house, where she

fixed me lunch. A short time later, her parents got home and welcomed me like I was their long-lost son.

"Do you have a place to stay tonight?" they wanted to know.

I thanked them but told them I had to be on my way. It felt wonderful to be treated so well. I was learning how to get along with people. I found that if you smiled, and were thoughtful and kind, and showed respect and concern for them, they would treat you the same way.

Well, before I knew it, a season passed, and it was wintertime again. I headed east just because I wanted to. I loved the freedom to move about when and where I wanted to go. I found myself in Cornwall, Connecticut. It was kind of cold out and would soon be dark, and I was walking along the street. A cop pulls up in his car and acts all friendly and everything, and then tells me to get in the back of his car.

I said, "What? I didn't do anything!"

He said, "I know you didn't. I'm just gonna take you down to the jail, get you some dinner, and let you spend the night. They got beds, and blankets, and everything."

Whoa, that cop didn't have to stop for me. He could have just kept going on down the road and nobody would have known the difference. He stopped and did a good thing for me, and I was grateful.

Next few months I banged around the New England states. Small states. In a car you could cover two or three states in a day, but I was in no hurry. So I did a lot of hitchhiking, long as the snow wasn't too deep. Never had any trouble hitchhiking. Seems like a lot of people of goodwill out there. They saw you before they decided to stop. So they sized you up and kind of knew a little bit about what they were getting into. Never had nothing but friendly conversation passing the time of day.

Suddenly, I got homesick. I missed Mama's cooking, the fried chicken and the mashed potatoes and gravy. I missed talking to Daddy. I missed my brothers and sisters. Only one thing left to do. I had not yet made it to the South. Carl had advised me against it, but it was one of the reasons I set out as a hobo—to know what it felt like to be in the South.

A campfire by the tracks

I hopped a freight car that took me as far as Virginia. I jumped out of that one and boarded a boxcar that was slated to leave in an hour for Alabama. Since the car wasn't moving, I scooted all the way to a dark corner in the back of the car. After a while the train was about to roll when, suddenly, a heavyset bull stepped up on the footstool and stuck his nose in the car. I might have still been okay, but then he did something most bulls don't do. Even though it was still daylight, he shined a flashlight into my dark corner.

"Well, lookie what we got here," he said. "Some punk kid looking for a lynching!"

Those words shot right through my heart. I had heard about lynchings all my life but was never threatened with one before.

He boosted his big belly up on the deck of the car and started scrambling to his feet. Trying to balance his whole fat body on his rounded midsection was a problem. The car lurched forward, jerking the fat man to his side. I saw him reach for that police baton Carl told me about.

"Ugh," he yelled. "I'm gonna beat the hell out of you!"

Adrenalin shot through my veins and I panicked to get out of there. I was a lot quicker than the fat bull, and I saw the path that I could use to scoot by him and get off that train. I flew out the open side of the car and landed on my feet but rolled to the side, cushioning my fall. The train picked up speed and clipped on down the track. As the last car passed me by, I remembered my knapsack—gone!

Overall, I had a wonderful life as a hobo, but this experience in the South told me that Daddy was right to get out of here, and I was glad to be doing the same thing.

As you know, I've lived a long time, and the older I get, the happier I am. Some of the fondest memories of my life are from the time I spent traveling the country as a hobo. I met warm and caring people, and the freedom I experienced in moving around the country represented to me the opposite of slavery. I could come and go as I pleased. No chains held me back. I could take responsibility for myself and be as independent as I wanted to be. I enjoyed those years.

Well, I'm seventeen now. Wouldn't trade hoboing around for anything, but time to go home and get on with my life.

Chapter 6

Life in the South

It was good to see the country, but I was glad to be home. Daddy has been taking me to the factory where he made parts for the Ford Motor Company. He's been showing me how to be a metalworker, to solder, weld, and do all kinds of work with my hands. I like it better than school, and I'm learning things that will help me make a good living in the future.

Mama has fixed the best dinners with the mashed potatoes, gravy, and butter, along with everything else she makes that I love. I can't imagine ever being late for dinner again. I know I am loved in my home, and that Mama and Daddy really want what is best for me. When I think about my brief taste of the South in that railroad car, where that bull wanted to beat me up and lynch me, I just can't get that out of my mind.

That man hated me without even knowing me. Is that what the South is like? I'm glad I didn't stay a minute longer, but I did some reading, and I want to share a little more family history, as well as some of what I've learned.

I was lucky to escape my one hostile confrontation in the South, and I'm glad I never *lived* there.

My father was James Edward Armistead, and being born in Virginia, he knew the South. My mother was Mary Alice Ford, born in Jamaica. She came to Virginia as a young girl. When my father and mother met and fell in love, they wanted to get married and raise a family. But my father, in his wisdom, knew life would be too hard for a black family in the South.

He decided to take his young wife north to New York. He

knew that the city was home to different kinds of people. There were Cubans, Puerto Ricans, Jews, Italians, Irish—they all lived there. He figured New York could just as easily handle a few more black people—and it wouldn't make a difference.

As it worked out, my father was at the head of a long line of what came to be known as the Great Migration. Between 1910 and 1940, one-and-a-half million Negroes left the South for greener pastures. For some it was just to find a better job. Some were in search of true freedom, an opportunity to live their lives without being under the thumb of the white man. This was their hope at the time. For some the general level of violence and prejudice was too strong in the South, and they thought they had a better chance in the North. And for others it was the outright fear of being lynched.

After several decades of lynchings, the Tuskegee Institute started keeping records in the early twentieth century, and a few years after that, the National Association for the Advancement of Colored People (NAACP) also kept records. The totals were close but not identical. These two well-respected organizations agreed that between the years of 1882 and 1968, over 4,700 people were lynched in the United States. Most were black, and most lynchings took place in the South.

The Tuskegee Institute and the NAACP probably didn't have the exact same figures on lynchings, because blacks had no standing in the community. Black life wasn't that important in this culture. Kind of like a dog got shot and was lying in the street. Some people take note of it, some don't. Doesn't really matter in the whole scheme of things, not in these parts. Who knows how many blacks were strung up with a rope or murdered any which way? One would be too many, that's for sure. But there were thousands.

When a lynching took place, it was important to the white man that it be publicized. The whole purpose of a lynching was not just to punish an *uppity* black and to mete out *justice,* as they called it, without due process. The main purpose was to keep the blacks subservient and maintain the upper hand through fear. The more people—black *and* white—around town who knew about the lynching and who witnessed it, well, the more effective it was to keep people in line.

The shame of the white man

One sickening part of a lynching was when target practice would break out. Whites in the crowd would fire shots at the body. At times hundreds of shots were fired into the corpse, as if to emphasize the worthlessness of the life just taken and the superiority of the takers. No doubt the rabble-rousers would have liked to take their potshots sooner, but none wanted to cut short the suffering of the victim.

To get a lasting effect from the lynching, whites started taking pictures of the victim and posed for pictures like they were celebrating a successful African safari, and I guess in some ways they were. I wonder if looking at the picture of a black man hanging from a tree, perfectly still, made it seem that this entire event was quiet and peaceful. They even started making postcards out of the pictures and sending them around. Some would cut off a body part and keep it for a souvenir. Can you imagine? It was a bad, bad time for the black man.

When they executed a black man, they always called it a lynching, but sometimes they believed that hanging from the end of a rope was too good for the black man. His crime was considered to be so bad in some way, especially if it involved the rape or murder of a white woman.

The lynching of Henry Smith was like that—Paris, Texas, February 1, 1893. With the Internet today, you can still read about the murder of Henry Smith. I'm not saying that Smith might not have deserved the death penalty, but he sure got no due process, no trial, no legal defense, no jury of his peers. Nothing like that. Even if he'd been put on trial, he wouldn't have had a jury of his peers. That's for sure.

The lynching of Henry Smith in Paris, Texas

Henry Smith was a seventeen-year-old kid who might have

been mentally retarded. He did odd jobs in Paris, Texas, and got arrested for something—don't know what. While he was in jail, a policeman beat him up. When he got out of jail, the story is that he took revenge for his beating by killing the three-year-old daughter of the cop, a little girl named Myrtle Vance.

The rumor got started that Henry raped little Myrtle, and this is how she was killed—by the physical trauma of that act. This is what enraged everybody. Well, Henry got out of town and apparently escaped on a freight train. He came from Arkansas, so a posse found him in a train station near Hope, Arkansas. They took him into custody, put him on a train, and headed back to Paris, Texas.

At every stop along the way, angry mobs gathered and were of no mind to wait for a trial. They wanted to string him up right away. But it was decided that Henry Smith would be burned alive back at the scene of the crime in Paris. I guess that was the only thing that kept people from ripping him right off the train and killing him on the spot.

When the train rolled into Paris, it was met by hordes of people full of rage, maybe upwards of ten to fifteen thousand. Hard to tell. Word had gotten out, and people came from all over. Texas Governor Jim Hogg tried to intervene and wired the local sheriff to take all means necessary to protect the prisoner from anarchy and vengeance. But the sheriff and his men were helpless.

The people paraded Henry through the town on some kind of animal cart and got to a place where they had built a wooden platform about ten feet high. They stripped him naked, tied him to a post on top, and tortured him for an hour.

It had become customary, when a white woman was raped or killed by a black man, for the family members to personally mete out the revenge, so the little girl's father and brother and a few other family members were up there on the platform, applying red-hot and white-hot irons to every square inch of Henry's body. They pierced and seared his private parts and put his eyes out. They say that his cries could be heard across the prairie.

Flesh was melting off his body, but he was still alive, so they doused him in kerosene and set him on fire like a human torch. When he finally gave up the ghost, his killers broke up his charred body parts and kept souvenirs of bones and anything left to show they had been part of this public spectacle.

Ida B. Wells, an activist and journalist who took a special interest in civil rights and especially lynchings, investigated the case of Henry Smith. In talking to witnesses, she discovered that Smith most likely did kill the little girl by strangling her—and he admitted to it after his capture, claiming he was drunk—but found it unlikely he committed a rape or any type of sexual assault, based on witnesses who saw the child's body.

In any case, Henry Smith was brutally executed through mob violence and outside the legal justice system. That's the way it was back in the day, and nobody did anything about it. Nobody was ever prosecuted. Got away scot-free. In all mob lynchings in those times, law enforcement just looked the other way. "Didn't recognize anybody at the scene," they would say. Or "People doing the lynching were of unknown origins." There you go.

Lynchings of blacks were more noticeable right after the Civil War ended in 1865. One of the first reasons for lynching a black man was to protect the white woman. White men were sensitive about black interaction with white women. They no longer had iron-clad control over the Negro. The black man had freedom, and that made the white man nervous—right down to a black man and a white woman walking past each other on the sidewalk. Did he brush up against her? Did he look at her the wrong way? Did he say something or give her a wolf whistle? Black men have been lynched for all of these offenses.

The black man had to be very slavish, like he wasn't even free. A bootlicker, a groveler, compliant and servile. Race-mixing was not something the white man would tolerate. Totally against southern tradition, at least when it was a black man with a white woman. The white man had had it this way for a long time, and this is the only way the white man was comfortable.

A black man could get lynched in the South for many reasons or for no reason at all. Accidentally bumping into a white person. Being disrespectful to a white person. Arguing with a white person. Acting suspiciously. Conducting himself with *independence of mind*. Lord, have mercy! What a shame if a black man thought for himself. It's a surprise any black people survived at all, living in the South like it was back in the day.

If a black man wanted to up his chances of getting lynched, let him sit down at the card table and gamble with the white man. He has just set the stage for argument and disagreement. Plus, the white man was of no mind to let the black man win or get something over on him. Even if he wins the card game, he was sure to lose the battle at the end of the rope. No way for the black man to walk away alive.

Another way for the black man to get in trouble was that he was now in competition with the white man in business. You see, the white man had the upper hand over the black man for centuries, and now all of a sudden the black man is set free and given the same opportunities—the right to vote, the right to own property, to have due process in the law. The black man was held down and subservient, but now had the same rights as the white man, and I think that scared the hell out of both sides.

All these years the white man had the benefit of the black man's free labor. But not anymore. Now, overnight, the black man could own his own farm, and work for himself, and compete against the white man. And the white man would have to pay wages to anyone who worked for him.

Now, it was hard for a newly freed slave to buy some land. They didn't have anything. But sometimes, a former slave owner would give an ex-slave a small piece of land to help him get started. Or they might strike up a deal so the former slave could work the land as a sharecropper or tenant farmer. In some parts of the South, they found that the number of lynchings increased at the end of the year when accounts had to be settled. We're talking the late nineteenth and early twentieth centuries.

Settling up money just seemed to bring out points of disagreement or contention. The black man may have done real well, and the white man didn't like it. Or the black man maybe wasn't ready to pay what the white man thought he was owed. After all, the black man didn't have any history of managing money, and there would be no tolerance or understanding on the part of the white man if he couldn't pay what was agreed exactly on time. Or there could have been a disagreement as to how much the black man owed, contract be damned. Or maybe there *was* no written contract. All sorts of ways to have misunderstandings.

And all the state and local laws required separate but equal public accommodations in the South. Buses, trains, restaurants, schools. Everything segregated, nothing integrated. These were the Jim Crow laws. Violating enough of these laws could get you lynched too.

So this was life in the South back in the day. Almost any infraction could cause the black man to be hanged. And yes, even women and children have swung from a tree at the end of a rope. Any man who has ever loved a woman, or any man or woman who has ever had a child, just think about that for a moment. Let that sink into your heart and your soul. No wonder the black man hated the white man.

My father was a wise man and made the best decision to raise his family in New York. If we'd have lived in the South, I don't think I'd be here at the age of ninety-seven talking about my good life.

Chapter 7

The Women in My Life

Daddy said taking off on the road would make a man out of me, and I believe he was right. I sure feel different now. I make my own decisions about coming and going. Mama understood this to an extent, but now that I'm home, she wanted me to show up for supper every night to be sure I'm okay.

Well, that wasn't always easy to do, especially if I'm out there hound-dogging around. I told Mama that if I show up for supper, she would know I'm there. If I didn't show up for supper, she would know I'm not coming. And as to whether or not I'm okay, just figure I'm okay. I can take care of myself.

I meant Mama no disrespect, but that's just the way it had to be now.

Other things had changed too. I used to go to church every Sunday with the family, and I just didn't feel like doing that now. Probably had to do with my experiences traveling the country and the freedom that I'd had.

I've told you that Daddy taught me lots of things, but one thing he never taught me nothing about was sex. I think that's one area I would have appreciated hearing from Daddy about. Not in a physical way so much but more like when it was appropriate, when to go ahead and when to run the other way. Things like that. With Daddy's values, he might have told me not to have sex with a woman until I was married to her. That's probably what he would have said, and that might not have worked too good for me at the time, not after everything I'd seen.

Bringing the entire family to church on Sundays was real

important to Mama and Daddy. One Sunday after I'd returned from my time out there as a hobo and I wasn't getting up for church, my older sister Bessie came into the boys' bedroom and threw water in my face to get me out of bed. Would have made Mama real happy for me to go to church with her, but I still wasn't gonna go. Bessie and me were yelling at each other by this time.

"What's going on in here?" Mama wanted to know.

"Just trying to get him out of bed so he'll go to church with you, Mama."

"Why won't you go to church with us, Sandy?" Mama asked. "Is it the preacher? You been around white folk so much maybe you'd rather go to a white church."

"No, Mama," I said. "I ain't gonna be no fly in the buttermilk!"

"Hmmph!" Mama said.

Now, I always seemed to get along with women. It was easy for me, like sliding down a snowy hillside. One morning I was sitting at the kitchen table and Mama walked in. I looked at her and said something like, "Mama, your hair sure looks pretty today." That seemed to surprise Mama, and she got a smile on and said to me, "Sandy, you could charm the birds right out of a tree."

One thing I like to do is tip my hat to a person when I meet them, especially the ladies. Makes them feel special. Daddy taught me that a long time ago. It's a sign of respect. People don't do that so much today, but that's okay. Doesn't mean I can't do it as a way of being polite. In fact, makes it stand out even more. Ladies seem to really appreciate it.

Since I'd been home, I met this girl who lived in the next apartment building over, another nine-story building. Her name was Mary. She was what I'd call *fine,* and I really liked spending time with her, if you know what I mean. But Mary lived with her Aunt Tilly, and her aunt sized me up real quick, and she didn't think I was a good influence on Mary. In fact she didn't like me at all, and I was forbidden from coming over to see her niece. She even alerted a couple of her friends who lived in apartments near the front door, and if they were to see me, they were told to run me off and tell her.

So that was the situation. But Mary was real fine and I just had to see that girl. So the only way I could get away with it was to jump from the edge of my roof to the edge of her roof, walk over to the other side, then lower myself down with a rope, and swing myself through the ninth floor open window to Mary's bedroom. That was a lot of work, but I felt it was worth it. And as strong and agile as I was, I could get by with it.

Now, Mary's aunt got off work at five o'clock each day and was walking up the stairs by 5:30. I always left no later than 5:15 so as not to create any kind of problem. Well, this one day I'm lollygagging along with my girl, and it was coming up on 4:30. All of a sudden, I hear some footsteps outside the door and then the jingle of keys in the door lock. *What the ...?*

I grabbed my shirt and my shoes and high-tailed it into auntie's bedroom, the only place I could see to hide. It was one way in, and one way out. I slid across the hardwood floor with my socks and dropped under the bed, clutching my shoes and my shirt in my arms. The low-hanging bedspread blocked the view of my heaving chest and my sorry ass.

Now, I'm trying to hush my breathing. Auntie walks into her room and sits down on her bed. A stiff wooden frame kept the springs from sinking down into my chest. Auntie throws off one shoe, then another. Next thing I know she takes off her work dress and tosses it on the floor. I could tell by the squeaking of the bed and the bulge in the mattress exactly where Aunt Tilly was sitting. I guess there was about one inch clearance near the head of the bed where I could see the stuff she had thrown on the floor. Then she walks over to her dresser, pulls out a squeaky drawer, and grabs some pajamas. And believe me, I wasn't peaking! *Lord have mercy!* She would *kill* me if she knew I was right there.

She walked out into the kitchen, leaving her bedroom door

open, and called Mary to come help her fix some supper. I'm laying still as a statue in Central Park. I don't dare come out from my hiding place. Even if she had shut her bedroom door, we're nine stories up and I'm not familiar with where her window leads, except outside and down. And besides, I couldn't be quiet enough to get out of there anyway without her knowing about it.

I am trapped under this woman's bed! After Auntie crawled under the covers for the night, I fell asleep for a little while, and it's a good thing I don't snore. I was quiet as a mouse under that lady's bed, but I heard every noise *she* made, I can tell you that. Well, I wake up in the dark of night with my bladder screaming for relief. I mean, I *gotta* go! No talking myself out of it.

Now, Aunt Tilly is in sweet, sweet dreamland, sawing logs to her heart's content. Ain't nothing gonna wake her up, that's for sure. I quietly pick up my shoes and my shirt and slide out from under her bed. Her door was ajar so I didn't have to mess with the door knob. Thank God for small favors. I pull the door open enough that I can slip through the opening. One inch to go. Wouldn't you know, that last inch chirps out a big squeak in the hinge. *Oh dear Lord!* Aunt Tilly snorts and rolls over on her side, her face pointing right at me. I'm quick-stepping down the hallway to Mary's room, not giving Auntie's eyelids a chance to open up. I slip my shirt and shoes on, open the window, and start climbing my rope.

Halfway to the roof, I hear Aunt Tilly call out, "Mary, Mary, you okay?"

I scramble to the top and pull up my rope. Just then Auntie sticks her head out the window. *Oh Lordy!*

Like I told you, Daddy was our teacher. Taught lots of good stuff about life—how to do the right thing, how to respect people, how to be independent. But that sex issue, never heard nothing about that. Maybe that's kind of an awkward subject, but I would have liked to be better prepared about that. You know—birth control, things like that. Never had any problems along that line, but it was always on my mind. As it was I had to learn the hard way on my own. Could be it's better that way. My time seeing the sights certainly broke the ice, but I would have rather not spent that time under Auntie's bed, that's for sure. Daddy never knew about that.

I remember one day I tried to bring a Puerto Rican girl home to meet the family. Mama stood right in the doorway, blocking the open space with her arm. Wasn't gonna have none of it. Wanted to keep the bloodline pure, I guess. Mama didn't realize how things were changing.

In the long run, women were always attracted to me. It came naturally. I liked women. I could make them laugh and smile. Women like to be treated well. One thing I could never stand is to see a man physically abusing a woman. I'm not a big guy, but I would always get in the middle if I saw a man doing that. I'd rather take the beating than see a woman get hurt.

Women like a man who is thoughtful and kind and sees things from their point of view, not just his own. Lots of men are blind to that. But a man's gotta show some strength. Gotta be tough enough to walk the edge a little bit, show some balls.

One time, during a period when I was single, I hung out at this bar, and the women flocked around me. One of them said to me, "I know what kind of man you are."

"Oh, you do, huh?" I said. "And how do you know that?"

"By the way you walk!"

"Hmmph!"

My first wife was Ruby. We were married for six years and had three children. I loved them all very much. But one thing I realized about Mama and Daddy's marriage is that they made it look so easy, but I found that it ain't that easy. Life gets in the way sometimes. Mama and Daddy were really in love, and they worked hard at making a good life for each other and a good home for us kids.

I'll show you how much my parents cared for each other. Two of my brothers were born the same year, and they weren't twins. Lawrence was born in January, and Hillary—a boy's name in those days—was born in December. I think that makes a pretty darn good statement about how my father felt about my mother. Couldn't keep his hands off of her. And I don't think she was complaining one bit.

Ruby and I were doing all right, except I had developed an interest in music and the clubs in Harlem. I played the drums and wanted to get more playing time. I would bring the drums to the Birdland Jazz Club on 1678 Broadway, just north of W. 52nd Street, for Art Blakely, a well-known drummer back in the day, and set them up for him. I wanted to spend more time learning from Art.

The Birdland Jazz Club back in the day

I loved being around the jazz legends who would come to the Birdland, stars like Miles Davis, Count Basie, Duke Ellington, Ella Fitzgerald, and so many more.

I would tap dance in the club with Billy Holiday and Bob Steele, and sometimes, to get in more practice, we'd dance even on the street corners. We'd set out a hat and people would toss in coins to show their appreciation. I was often mistaken for Sammy Davis Jr. He came to the club a lot, and we were about the same size. His father was black and his mother Puerto Rican. My father was black and my mother Jamaican. I never minded too much if people smiled and called me Sammy.

Well, I had three kids at home, but I wanted to spend too much time away. My time at the club even cut my work hours short, and Ruby wouldn't hear of that. She wanted a man who spent more time at home and brought home a steady paycheck to take real good care of those kids, and she was right. So we divorced, and even though I didn't see as much of the kids as she'd like, I always made decent enough money to provide for them.

I moved to California in the early '60s. I enjoyed life in L.A. and Hollywood. As a single man I definitely didn't follow in my Daddy's footsteps. I drove a red, '61 Cadillac convertible with wide fins. It was a flashy car and attracted more than my share of good-looking ladies. My friends started calling it the *pimpmobile* because I was rarely seen driving it without a woman by my side. I guess you could say I was a low-down dirty rascal.

I remember one night standing on the corner of Hollywood and Vine, waiting for the light to change, and a slow-moving car with open windows turning the corner passed right by me, and the passenger said, "How's it going, nigger?" It was a black man who said it, and he probably meant it as a term of familiarity, like a badge of honor for traveling the same path through life, kind of like sharing the load. Black men sometimes called each other that name, seeking some kind of common ground.

If it had been a white man who'd said it, it would have

been an insult, which happens from time to time. But I don't pay no never mind. Just means that he showed his own ignorance, not mine.

After being single for a while in L.A., I met and fell in love with Gertie. We married and had a good eighteen-year marriage until she got ill and passed away. We enjoyed life together, and I cared for her every day during her sickness. I really missed Gertie.

I am currently married to my third wife, Vanessa. We have been married fifteen years. She is a good wife and a bit younger than me. I am very happy to be married to her. We share a wonderful love. She takes good care of me, and I take good care of her. Vanessa is a fine-looking woman, if you know what I mean.

Chapter 8

Drafted

I was twenty years of age when the Japanese attacked Pearl Harbor on December 7, 1941. Within a year all men between the ages of eighteen and sixty-four had to register for the draft. After that, we were checked out according to our ability to serve in the military. The draft boards took into consideration our skills, occupation, family situation, health, and how we might best serve. We were accepted based on the military's needs and our ability to meet those needs. I didn't have to read about any of this stuff, because I lived it.

Women also helped a lot with the war effort but were not drafted. Women volunteered and served as pilots, nurses, factory workers, and food growers. They collected much-needed items like copper, rubber, and sugar. Some planted gardens that came to be known as *Victory Gardens* so that enough food could be put into K-rations and sent overseas for the troops. We wouldn't have been nearly as successful if it wasn't for all that the women did.

One thing I'll never forget is how America was so united during the time of the war. We operated like one. We had a single goal—to win the war. I don't believe we could have accomplished that without being unified.

We had a great leader in President Roosevelt. The day after the attack on Pearl Harbor, he said, "No matter how long it may take us to overcome this premeditated invasion, the American people in their righteous might will win through to absolute victory." How strong and inspiring he was.

In the early part of 1943, I was drafted, along with millions of other men, into the U.S. military. My branch was the army. I went to basic training in Petersburg, Virginia. I was trained in infantry and shipped out to Italy and Germany. I was prepared for combat, but I didn't see any action at all.

I loaded and unloaded trucks and trains and hoisted bombs up into the bellies of fighter planes. Lots of hard, physical labor. Right or wrong, it seemed to me that the black man was held back from actually being part of the war effort. I don't know if the U.S. government didn't believe in the black man, that he could be trusted to make good decisions and be effective as a soldier, or if they didn't want to give the black man any credit for contributing to the success of the war.

Whatever way it was, the black man had a lot of servant roles. We could serve coffee in the officer's mess, but to charge up the hill with a rifle and a bayonet, you didn't see much of that.

The heavy lifting gave me a back injury, and I spent two months in the hospital. My bed was next to a white soldier named Sullivan, who had a different kind of injury—shrapnel from a bombing overseas. He had developed sepsis and they were trying to overcome the infection and heal the wound so he could be useful in serving our country. We both were working on getting well.

In the many weeks we were together, we shared a lot of experiences, mostly about family and childhood and our plans for the future.

Finally, after two months of trying to heal up, one of the doctors, a captain, came to me and told me he was sorry to say, but they weren't going to be able to use me and were going to send me home with an honorable, medical discharge. I always had a thought in the back of my mind that I might be killed in the war and have my life cut short at a young age.

My early discharge meant that I wouldn't be killed in the war, and I was happy for that. But in another way I was very disappointed because I loved my country, and I wanted to fight for it and contribute to the war effort. So it was a mixed bag for me.

The day they released me, I was standing beside my bed, packing up my belongings, and Sullivan in the bed next to me told me some things I could never forget. "When I get home," he said. "I'm going to tell my parents what liars they are."

"What do you mean?" I said.

"They told me nothing but lies about you," he said. "They don't even know you. They never talked to a black person. I don't think they've ever *known* a black person, so they don't know anything about you. You want the same things in life that I want. You want to have a wife and a family. You want a good job to provide for them. You want peace, and health, and happiness. You're no different than I am."

"Well, I'm sure they didn't mean no harm," I said.

"They shouldn't try to tell me things about black people if they don't know what they're talking about," he said. "Do you know, they tried to tell me that black people have tails like monkeys?"

Seventy-five percent of what people are taught about others are lies. People hate because they are *taught* to hate. They hate people they don't even know, based on things that aren't even true. They hate you before they see you.

I didn't know what to say about monkey tails. I had heard that a time or two, but it sounded so ridiculous I didn't know if people really thought that or if it was just something to say. I do remember shortly after the war they held a victory march in New York City. Soldiers marched by from all branches of the military, wearing their dress uniforms, and people on the sidewalk with me would bend over and look down trying to catch a glimpse of the black man's tail.

"They got it tucked up under the coat," one man said.

"Yep, that's what it is," another said.

"Do you really think the black man's got a tail?" I jumped in. "I ought to drop my pants and shove my black ass right in your face. Then you'd know for sure!"

Some pushing and shoving got going right there. People joined in and we got separated from one another, but I kept watching the victory march. I was still proud to be an American, and I enjoyed watching the soldiers from all branches of the armed services march by in their dress uniforms. I felt a strong part of it, even though I wasn't able to fight with them.

Common sign of the times

I'll never forget when, a few years later, I was in Virginia and I wanted to go into this café and get a cup of coffee. I walked in the front door, and the manager rushed right over and told me they didn't serve my kind in here.

"My kind?" I said. "My *kind*? I served in the army for my country during World War II. I was willing to lay down my life. And you can't serve me a cup of coffee?"

"Maybe you did, but we don't care nothing about that in here!"

The manager showed me the door. I had my say but I felt powerless to get that coffee. It would have been so good to sit at the counter and drink that cup of coffee like any other man.

I left the building like he told me, but I stayed outside in the parking lot, walking around, thinking about what had just happened. I was angry and frustrated and sad. So many feelings because what this man did was just so wrong.

He didn't see an American veteran. He didn't see a good man with a good mind and heart who would help other people.

He couldn't see a decent person. All he could see was a black man, a man who didn't deserve the common courtesy of a seat at the counter to enjoy a cup of coffee, all because of the color of his skin.

A police car showed up, I guess 'cause I didn't leave from outside and the manager must have called them.

"You're gonna have to get off the property," the officer said.

"But I didn't do anything wrong."

"I know you didn't, but you might as well leave. It'll just cause a lot of trouble if you don't."

So I left.

In the military you meet people from all over the country, sometimes all over the world. People of different races and colors and religions. You got to learn to get along with people. Give people the benefit of the doubt. Take the time to understand them and get to know them. That's what happened to me and Sullivan in the hospital. We were kind of thrown in together like that by the military, but it turned out to be a good thing. In the shelter of our homes, growing up, we didn't get to know people of different races. We were just with our own. This was a good experience for both of us.

That evening I got to thinking that people can be conditioned to believe or feel about others in a certain way— many times without even realizing it. The black man has a bad experience with the white man and can't think about the white man in any other way but bad. Just expects bad things to happen. The white man has a bad experience with the black man and can't think any way about the black man but bad. It's hard to overcome.

But you got to give people a chance. Take the time to get to know a person. Learn to get along with people. Don't try to be macho and take control of everyone and every situation. Just be yourself.

I have a grandson who doesn't like being black. He has

figured out that life is not so good as a black man, so he tries to pass for white. All of his friends are white, and he tries to be like them. He lives in a dream world, pretending he is white.

Reminds me of a guy I used to work with. He tried to pass for white the whole time he worked in this factory. He believed it gave him better job security, and he was right. Now, he knew that I knew what he was doing, and he begged me not to tell the boss. I had no reason to, so we got along fine. But others knew also. We'd go just outside the building on a break and recite this together: "Looks white, light and bright. Two drops short of white, so not quite." And we'd bend over and laugh and slap our knees. I think it's better to just be who you are. Be genuine, without pretense.

When it comes to others, accept them as *they* are. People who know me think that I'm a nice person, but I'm not nice to everybody. I'm nice to people I like and respect and *want* to get along with. But if I don't like or respect someone, I keep my distance. I don't believe in hanging around people who can put you in the ground. You gotta be real.

Color doesn't have to be such a big deal. If you think about it, the heart is neutral as far as color. If you examined a black man's heart and a white man's heart, I'll bet you couldn't tell the difference. It's just a thin layer of pigment on the skin that is noticeable and separates us because we let it and because it reminds us of the past.

One day I'm sitting on a bench in Central Park feeding the pigeons. There was a family across the way over on the grass having a picnic. Two little girls, five or six years old, were tossing a ball around. The ball came rolling over to me, so I reached down and picked it up.

"Well, hello there," I said, ready to hand the ball over. Now, one girl was white and one was black, and their smiles were wide as the East River.

"What's your name?" I said to the pudgy little white girl.

"Linda. Wanna know what my daddy calls me?"

"What does your daddy call you?"

"Princess Butterball!"

I turned to the black girl, but before I could open my mouth, she said, "Wanna know what my daddy calls *me*?"

"What does your daddy call *you*?" I asked.

"Chocolate!" she said. Then she giggled.

These two little girls didn't know they were different, because they weren't. They just knew laughter and acceptance. They couldn't see the color of their skin, but they could feel the love in their hearts.

I'll bet if all people were the same shade of tan or gray, there would still be trouble between people because it would come down to power. One group wants to have control over the others. But power like that can become a sickness.

A man's heart is where you find integrity, courage, and love. Character and commitment. That's what matters. I remember reading in a book about life by Victor Frankl. He said there's only two races of people in the world, the decent and the indecent. That's the way I see it. And he knows what he's talking about. He survived Nazi concentration camps.

And about that blue-eyed devil? Do you know that I have a great-grandson who is blond-haired and blue-eyed? Color ain't nothing. After four generations of intermarrying and having children, colors change and don't matter one bit. What we want to see is what's in a man's heart. That's what counts.

Dr. Martin Luther King knew this. In his famous speech outside the Lincoln Memorial, he said something like this. He said, "I have a dream that my four little children will one day live in a nation where they will not be judged by the color of their skin but by the content of their character."

There are some racists scattered all across this planet, and no doubt, there are some in America. But did you hear that America elected a black president? I never thought I would live to see that day. I had to stick around a long time, but I did finally see it happen. So I would prefer to call America the land of opportunity rather than a place of abuse and crime. You don't elect a black president unless an awful lot of people get together in the election process and agree this should happen.

Back in the day, America was a pretty rough place, and a lot of people suffered outside the law. But you know, America is a different place today. I've seen the changes. As a country we're not perfect. We go astray for a while and then we make corrections. All in all I would say America is the most praiseworthy country in the world. We try to be fair to those who live within our borders, and we try to help the whole world.

We offer freedom and opportunity and justice. Think about it. What do you want to do with your life that you can't do in America? Focus on this, not injustices of the past. None of us can change the past. All we can do is move forward and create a better country and a wonderful life.

And never forget this. People from all over the world are trying to get to America. They must know something! Those who have successfully immigrated here have enjoyed the freedoms and opportunities this country has to offer, and some have achieved great material wealth beyond their wildest imaginations. In my mind there is no other country on the planet that has this much to offer. I am so happy—and proud and thankful—to be an American!

Chapter 9

On the Job

After my hoboing days were over, Daddy helped me get a real job with a real company. I was now working in a steel mill in Stamford, Connecticut, making auto parts for Henry Ford. It was the late 1930s. My father and two of my brothers worked there. Daddy taught me metal working over the years, so it was easy for me to step in at the steel mill.

Daddy always said a man should get real good at what he does, and to do that he should be working at something he likes. I always enjoyed being a metal worker, bending steel into shape, welding and riveting, being outdoors working on something that is bigger than life and important to a lot of people.

I was making $27.75 a week. It was close to 75 cents an hour, and they paid you in cash. No income taxes for us in those days. It doesn't sound like much by today's wages, but with rent at $11.75 a month, and a loaf of bread for five cents, we had plenty of money. We had nothing to compare it with. It was what it was. But with that kind of money, and Daddy making even more, we could buy whatever we needed.

Another place where I worked that was plenty dangerous but never scared me was the high rises that were built in New York in the 20th century. There are hundreds of skyscrapers with more planned and more under construction. Some are hundreds of feet high, some over a thousand.

I worked on lots of buildings that nobody would recognize by name, but the most famous structure I personally worked on stands just above five hundred feet tall in Manhattan: the United

Nations building overlooking the East River. We started work on it in 1949, after the war, of course, and finished in 1952. That was quite an accomplishment.

Where's OSHA when you need them?

I was one of those guys up on the beams welding rivets. I had a supervisor who didn't like heights, and he was always sending me up to where he had just been to get what he'd left behind. He didn't go much higher than the fifth floor, and he wasn't about to make an extra trip.

In those days a man had to look out for his own safety in all kinds of jobs. We didn't have a government agency like OSHA looking out for people. Sometimes, there was an effort by another group, maybe an insurance company, to make things safer, but I don't think anybody knew exactly what to do about safety with people working up so high. For a while they tried to set up some netting below the beams where men were working, but that seemed to fade out. Probably hard to catch a guy in a net.

My bosses tried me out to see if I could handle the heights, and I could. I was nimble and sure-footed and could climb with the best of them. I never felt afraid. Not everybody could handle it. A lot of men over six feet tall in those days were kind of awkward and clumsy, and you didn't need that a couple of hundred feet in the air.

I remember one day when we were up pretty high, sitting on a beam, eating lunch. The winds were stiff as always and shifting around quite a bit. I turned to my right to say something to George, but George wasn't there. Just an empty space where he had sat. The man sitting on the other side of George saw him slide off the beam. White as a sheet—he could barely talk.

I learned three things about safety on the high rise. One, don't look down. Nothing to be gained by looking down. Keep your eyes on the things around you so you can keep yourself stable. Two, lean into the wind, but don't lean too hard. Winds shift. And three, you drop a sandwich, better let it go. Don't lunge. Live to eat another day. A man's safety truly is in his own hands.

I learned a lot from work and had many different kinds of jobs. After the United Nations project, I worked on 14th Street in New York City, building RCA products. It was the early 1950s and the marketplace was hot. We built radios, phonographs (later called record players), speakers, and vacuum tubes—airtight little tubes of glass with a steel base containing electrical components that would become standard equipment in the operation of television sets. And yes, we also manufactured a lot of those— televisions.

What a fast-moving market that was. They had individual franchise stores jam-packed with product—names like Zenith, Sylvania, and Magnavox. Then, just to be sure nobody missed out, they sold their products in the big department stores of the day like Sears, Two Guys, Macy's, and many others. We couldn't make them fast enough. The television was sweeping the nation, and word was every household would have a TV before long.

It was fun to be part of the design and development of a brand new product. We were on the cutting edge of a new industry, and we could see from the schematics how quickly things were changing, that the television set was going to be huge. But we really had no idea how much it would affect our lives.

Working at RCA was one of the safer jobs I ever had.

Most of my jobs took place in loud, noisy places— factories, mills, construction sites, and ships. Nothing was quiet with the pounding of hammers, the clashing of steel plates against heavy equipment, the pouring of molten steel, and the roaring of fast-moving machinery.

I'm a slight man, standing a bit under five-and-a-half-feet tall, but I stand straight, arms cocked outside my frame because my biceps have been developed over a lifetime of work. All my days I have worked with my hands and arms. I never sat behind a desk. That may be the reason I have lasted into my tenth decade.

Working with steel can be dangerous, and a man had to be careful to keep himself alive. If he wasn't paying attention, there wasn't much hope for him. Fast-moving, powerful machinery is unforgiving.

I've seen men get an arm caught in rollers feeding steel into a cutter. That's the end of the arm, and maybe the end of a man's life. The man's scream grabs everybody, even over the roar of the machinery. Someone has to hit the kill switch to stop the pull.

I've seen men get their shirt caught in a machine like that. It either rips the shirt off their back, or if there's no give in the shirt, it breaks their back. Whichever gives out first is where the damage is done, so a man's got to be careful in the factory.

Sometimes, a man had to work on a machine where a steel plate was being punched out of a larger sheet of metal. The plate that was being formed was obviously a smaller piece of a particular shape with the function of holding a part of the structure in place. In this process, sometimes a man's hand or fingers get in the way, and when that happens, they are gone in the blink of an eye.

I saw one man lose his fingers like this. The pressure of the punch was so great it severed the four fingers of his right hand, but because the glove was of softer material and had some give to it, the glove was intact, and the man's fingers were still in the glove.

I worked on a slitter machine, cutting copper into various lengths and sizes. There were two men, one to push the copper, one to cut. If the two didn't work together smoothly, or if the timing was off, fingers could be cut off. Working in the factory wasn't for sissies.

Molten steel was poured into huge vats and formed into shapes to become parts of the structure of whatever we were building—smaller parts for cars and sometimes bigger parts for ships. I wouldn't say it was common, but every now and then someone working above the vat controlling the pour would slip and fall into the liquid steel. You would see a pinkish mist rise above the container and the man was gone. It was a horrible thing, but the death was immediate. No suffering, just instant annihilation. Like a drop of sweat on a red-hot pile of coals.

Out of respect for the man and his family, the company would not use that steel in construction but would bury that portion of the steel in a hole in the ground, giving the man the best burial they could.

This type of work was dangerous, but that didn't stop a man from wanting the job. Had to have the job to support his family. When a man needs a job, he can overcome fears and doubts if he's given the chance. He can even learn to get along with people he might otherwise choose to avoid.

This was one of the frustrations of the day. The black man walks into the company office and asks the white boss for a job. Now, keep in mind, the white boss was usually sitting on a high, boosted-up chair. Looked like a throne or something. It could be intimidating.

"We're not hiring anybody right now," the boss says.

Five minutes later the white man walks in to see the boss and asks for a job. Gets hired right on the spot. What's the black man to do? The black man needs the job just as much as the white man does, but it's so easy to turn him away. The black man was intimidated by the white man because the white man had the power and could punish the black man. If the white man blackballed the black man, he had no chance to get a job anywhere in town. And the black man didn't have the right to speak out. If he did, the white man had the attitude, *How dare you approach me like that!*

Even on the job. The black man is working on a welding project, and while his back is turned, the white man comes along and turns up the heat on the welding machine. Makes the black man's work look shabby and inferior, and the white man once again looks superior. The black man calls the white man a redneck and a honky. And you know what the white man called us. And hatred festered and grew. And the black man had to bite his tongue and keep the peace and be respectful to the white man, and it didn't set too well in his soul.

I saw a man walking the streets of New York after the war, wearing what we used to call a sandwich-board sign over his shoulders. Front and back he had painted:

> **I know 3 trades**
> **I speak 3 languages**
> **I fought for 3 years**
> **I have 3 children and**
> **No work for 3 months**
> **But all I want is one job**

It was not always easy for the black man to find a job.

Sometimes, dangers at work came along by total surprise. I was working as a welder on a tanker at the Todd Shipyard in Brooklyn. I went down into the hold, about ten feet below deck level. As I'm welding rivets down there, some workers came along and placed a cap on the hold, a steel piece that looked like a manhole cover, and they closed up the opening on the deck. Then they began to weld it shut.

I scrambled up to the opening in the deck as fast as I could.

I started yelling for all I was worth and began banging with my fist on the cover. My hand made no sound at all against the heavy steel disc that sealed the hold, and they couldn't hear my screams. So I grabbed a hammer from my tool belt and pounded away. They heard that and cut through the small part of the cover they had already sealed and opened it up. The sunlight flooded in like the life-giving tonic it is, and I crawled out into the fresh air. I will never forget that day and my escape from what would have become my tomb in the hold of that tanker.

Daddy always insisted that a man had to have the skills to do a job that was necessary in the workplace so he could be hired to make decent money on a regular basis. Someone without any skills looking for a job is in a sad situation.

The boss man says, "Can you weld?"

"No, I ain't a welder," the man says.

"Can you cut steel or bend iron?

"No, I ain't an iron worker."

"Can you cook so you could work as a chef?"

"No, I can't cook."

"Well, what *can* you do?"

"Well, I don't know, but I'm a hard worker."

The best job this man can be offered is to haul away the trash or clean up the yard. Now there's nothing wrong with that. There is honor in all honest work. But how much money can he expect to make? He will be at the bottom of the pay grade, and he is the easiest to replace. Anyone on two legs can take his job and do the same work.

When I think about it, most of the money that I made and the benefits that I received came from highly paid, regular employment. No question about it. Oh, I had some *side projects*, I'll call them. I had a criminal mind when it came to making money. I could see the schemes and the scams, the angles and the dangles, and how they could work, but I never crossed the line too far because I didn't want anyone to get hurt. And I didn't want to get myself killed. You've always got to consider the risk, you know?

Some of the things that I did to make money would not be approved of by my daddy. You probably already know that. He was very straight, by the book, and would never step over the line.

Sometimes, I *would* step over the line, but even then I kept Daddy's principles in mind. Daddy said, "Always take responsibility for what you did, *because you did it!*"

So in the end, the responsibility will always fall on you. That means you have to weigh the risk. If things don't work out, what do you stand to lose? Can you afford to lose it? You *will* have pay the price, you know.

I guess it would be fair to call me a conniver when it came to making money. I had the ability to pretend that I didn't see the wrongdoing of what someone did. And if I didn't see it, it seemed like I approved of it. That's what you call *conniving.* It let me get close enough to the action to get a slice of the pie, if possible.

After the war, in New York, I rented a large house. I set up the first floor like a bar with a nice big counter, some stools, tables and chairs, and a good supply of liquor. The kitchen was a few steps away. The bars closed at 2:00 AM, but you know, when people are drinking and having a good time, they don't want to go home. They want to keep having a good time.

So I opened up *Easter Island,* my own personal bar in my house, that was open from 2:00 AM to 7:00 AM. I hired a couple of bartenders and waitresses and a cook—and people flocked to my place. Part of the fun might have been that we did this with no licenses or permits. I made a good chunk of change for a couple of years, and the risk was nothing to worry about.

In the early '60s I moved to Southern California. Guess I never could forget how beautiful that State was, even in the wintertime. Found work as an iron worker and established my base. But you know, after the JFK assassination, as the '60s moved forward, it was the craziest decade I had ever seen. Demonstrations against the Vietnam War, flower children, pot smokers, more assassinations, and riots. Lots of craziness.

And something else going on—the sexual revolution. So I opened up a swingers' club, one of the first of its kind in L.A. With a membership fee of $500 per couple, I was making a lot of money. Even sold a love potion.

About that time a friend of mine was managing a large warehouse for a big company in L.A. Some drug dealers came by one day and asked him if they could store some cocaine in there between shipments. There was plenty of empty space, that was for sure. So without thinking too much about it, he said okay.

I asked him, "How much are you getting for letting them do that?"

"Uh, nothing," he said.

He could tell from the look on my face what I thought about that arrangement.

"You could have gotten $800 a month easy, don't you think?" I said. "They wouldn't have missed it." There goes my criminal mind again.

The Good Book says that the love of money is the root of all kinds of evil. I've seen it in my life. I always had money in my pocket. I was never a millionaire, but I believe I could have been if I'd have set my mind to it. Guess I never believed it would be worth the price I'd have to pay.

Chapter 10

What I Learned from Sandy Armistead
(the author's perspective)

It was a pleasure meeting and speaking with Sandy Armistead over the several months we worked on his story. We talked about life, family, work, women, and power.

Certain periods in our history were exceedingly dark. Back in the day the white man had power over the black man. When one group of people has power over another group, abuses can and often do occur. Slavery gave almost 100% control over the enslaved. For a hundred years after our country outlawed slavery, power still reigned over the black man through Jim Crow laws, lynchings, and abuses of all kinds outside the law.

Through all of this, Sandy Armistead learned to get along with many different kinds of people. He was slow to take offense and quick to forgive. He was charitable whenever possible and freely gave the benefit of the doubt. He took responsibility for himself and refrained from blaming others. Sandy was not a perfect man, but when he erred, he acknowledged it.

Sandy taught me that the white man and the black man need to switch the glasses through which they view the world. The white man looks at almost unlimited opportunity. He knows all doors are open to him. He is accepted in society. If he works hard, he can succeed and enjoy the fruits of his labor. He truly has the opportunity to attain *life, liberty, and the pursuit of happiness.*

But most white men don't seem to have awareness of the suffering of the black race. The white man acts like nothing happened. No slavery. No lynchings. No Jim Crow laws. No abuse outside the law. And no empathy.

The black man, to the contrary, is very much aware of the suffering of his race, almost to the exclusion of seeing genuine opportunities available to him now. Many black men walk around ruminating on the injustices of the past. What we think about makes a difference in what we do and who we become. And many black men become frustrated, discouraged, and angry. Some feel like *what's the use in trying?*

On this subject, Sandy taught me this: let the white man educate himself on the suffering of the black race. This book is a good start. Let the white man, as much as possible, place himself and his family in the shoes of the black man. Let him realize the mountain the black man has had to climb. Let him develop empathy and compassion for the journey of the black man in a white man's world.

And to the black man, let him remember the past, the cruelty that happened to his ancestors, the injustices, the bigotry, the discrimination. But let him not dwell on it. Instead, let the black man count his blessings. Focus on the opportunities available today to change lives. Become a better person. Develop skills that are needed in the marketplace and for personal development. Become more valuable. Let the black man become the best he can be in all areas of life.

All people, black and white, men and women, young and old, should develop an attitude of gratitude. Things to be thankful for are our measure of health, our friends, family, freedom, and the reality of the opportunities afforded us when we live in America.

Times change, but some people remain the same, looking at the wrong things. Doors are open today to hard-working people of all races.

Love and forgiveness are the key. All adversity can be overcome through love and forgiveness.

Thanks, Sandy, for the opportunity to see things, even for a little while, through your eyes.

May God bless America!

Epilogue

*Would you change anything about your life?

There were things that I endured at the time that I would rather have not experienced—like the time I was almost caught under Auntie's bed—but as I look back now, I learned from all of it, and it combined to make me who I am, so I wouldn't change a thing.

*What do you think of millionaire athletes who will not stand for the National Anthem?

I think they're out of their minds. Sports and capitalism gave them the opportunity to become successful beyond their wildest imaginations. Gratitude and respect for the sacrifices that have been made should be foremost in their minds. That's what I think.

*In fairness, the athletes who will not stand state they mean no disrespect to the flag. They say they are protesting due to *inequality.*

Inequality? How free do you have to be to be free? What is it you want to do with your life that you can't do in America?

*What is your attitude toward the United States of America?

It's not perfect, but it's the best country on this planet. It's the best place we'll know until we get to heaven. I love my country, and I am so glad to be born in America.

*What about the immigration problems?

I guess we have immigration problems because lots of people want to live here. That says something good about our country. But the fact is that we do have to set boundaries and conditions for coming here and becoming a citizen. To not do so is to endanger our current citizens and jeopardize our quality of life. Seems obvious to me.

*Do we need new laws in this country?

We got lots of laws. Laws about fairness, laws about equality, laws about opportunity, laws about boundaries. We just gotta start following them and enforcing them.

*What do you feel about the Second Amendment?

I believe that all men and women have a right to protect themselves and their families. I have a shotgun beside my bed. If somebody broke into my house, they'd be dead. And I wouldn't feel bad about it.

*Will the different races ever get along?

We can't change the world except by changing ourselves. We are the only ones we can actually change. I believe that love and forgiveness are the key. We cannot change the past. But if we can love and forgive one another, we can move forward and create new relationships and build trust and strong bonds. If we can't, we might as well live in 1935 in the South. And that's what a lot of people are doing.

Young black kids are angry at things they don't even understand. They're focused on the wrong things. Focus on the opportunities you have, not the injustices of the past. And if there are injustices today, learn the facts and make them known. Don't march and call for blood. Society will not respect that. And you may say that you don't care whether they respect it or not, but you want to be affective, don't you? If you want to affect change, you must remain under control, like our Brother Martin did. It's a long hard fight, but you know that progress has been made. And I believe we can get the rest of the way.

*What is your advice on how to get along with people?

Keep on the good side of people. Love and respect them, and they will love and respect you. See things from their perspective. Don't try to be a hard ass. Don't try to always have your own way. Like my father always said, follow the Golden Rule. Do unto others as you would have them do unto you. Have you ever tried it? It sounds so simple, but if you haven't tried it, you don't know how effective it is. It is simple, and I believe life is best lived in a simple way.

*Can a black man really make it in America today?

Let me tell you something. Immigrants who come here dirt poor make it really big. And so can anyone who was born and raised here. There is nothing holding anyone back except their own limited thinking and lack of effort. If a person sets their eye on the goal and refuses to be deterred, they can get where they want to get in America. To think otherwise is a myth.

*What is your religion?

I am a Christian, and I am so thankful to live in a country where I am free to worship and practice my religion.

Patriotism comes early

About the Author

Dwight Norris is a teacher, writer, and speaker. His first novel, *The Gentleman Host*, features a serial killer who throws middle-aged women off cruise ships. In his second novel, *My Name is Inferno*, a cruise ship in the Caribbean is overtaken by pirates. Dwight's third novel, *Johnny McCarthy*, leaves the sea and takes readers to Matewan, West Virginia, in the 1920s and depicts the hand-to-mouth lives of coal miners and their families trying to eke out a living in difficult times.

Dwight likes many forms of writing and, in addition to his novels, he has two screenplays to credit, as well as a dozen or so short stories, sundry poems, and quotations. He is the father of two adult children and lives in Southern California.

Contact Dwight at dwightedwardnorris@gmail.com

Photograph Permissions

Page 7: *The reason I was often late for dinner*
https://commons.wikimedia.org/wiki/File:Black_children_pla
ying_leap_frog_in_a_Harlem_street,_ca._1930_-_NARA_-
_541880_.jpg

Page 14: *Competition right down the street*
https://www.bing.com/images/search?view=detailV2&ccid=A
rGHMd46&id=E07C97DCEF2BB0C93A91A4C296A586047A97328C
&thid=OIP.ArGHMd460MgJBjVCOu7WqAHaKd&mediaurl=https%
3a%2f%2fc.pxhere.com%2fphotos%2f19%2f6b%2fvintage_photo
_old_street_shoe_shine_shoes_people-1043561.jpg!d&exph=16
96&expw=1200&q=negroe+shoeshine+boy&simid=60798672987
7704446&selectedIndex=60&qft=+filterui%3alicenseType-Any&c
blr=sbi&ajaxhist=0

Page 18: *The gangs of New York*
By The Library of Congress - https://www.flickr.com/photos
/library_of_congress/79_85821930/, No restrictions, https://com
mons._wikimedia.org/w/index.php?curid=53643275

Page 26: *Never the same again*
https://www.google.com/search?q=images+of+slavery&tbm=
isch&source=lnt&tbs=sur:fc&sa=X&ved=0ahUKEwjZn8-Y16ffAhW
HJTQIHbQ2CVsQpwUIIA&biw=1679&bih=1031&dpr=1#imgrc=M
EWYzvRmIYh8ZM:

Page 28: *A terrible existence*
https://www.google.com/search?tbm=isch&source=hp&biw=
1679&bih=1031&ei=-AMYXLDeFIyw0wKKyK3ICw&q=images+of+

slavery&oq=images+of+slavery&gs_l=img.3..0l8j0i5i30l2.5282.73
04..7525...0.0..0.97.1394.17......1....1..gws-wiz-img.....0.gWmIeoX
CQhU#imgrc=odaiSoovReHNUM:

Page 30: *Coffled together*
https://www.google.com/search?biw=1679&bih=1031&tbs=s
ur%3Afc&tbm=isch&sa=1&ei=yQUYXNLxBrS70PEPnrSF0AM&q=i
mages+of+slavery&oq=images+of+slavery&gs_l=img.3.. 35i39j0l7j
0i5i30l2.6524.28408..28679...0.0..0.100.1308.16j1......1....1..gws-
wiz-img.......0i67.Dxji1snzGvk#imgrc=ydcdOgdbXX2PyM:

Page 32: *A child's grief as a slave*
https://www.pinterest.com/pin/315674255101818278/?lp=tr
ue

Page 33: *No way to escape*
https://www.pinterest.com/pin/10836855328661041/

Page 43: *A campfire by the tracks*
https://www.google.com/search?tbm=isch&source=hp&biw=
1679&bih=1031&ei=EsMWXM2PC7yq0PEPtami-AQ&q=HOBOS&o
q=HOBOS&gs_l=img.3..0l10.2051.2606..2766...0.0..0.108.440.3j2.
.....1....1..gws-wiz-img.....0.97P1j9VhLmA#imgrc=-RFbULmog2KZi
M:

Page 47: *The same of the white man*
https://www.bing.com/images/search?view=detailV2&ccid=l6
p4X2EC&id=A99129A225366B8E3349B084CF8F2C23A8B1B55C&t
hid=OIP.l6p4X2ECMOxve2wdPwBzogHaEK&mediaurl=https%3A%
2F%2Fibw21.org%2Fwp-content%2Fuploads%2F2018%2F04%2F
why-america-must-atone-for-its-lynchings.jpg &exph=512&expw
=910&q=photographs+of+lynchings+of+negroes&simid=6080361
56335132315&selectedindex=539&ajaxhist=0&vt=0&eim=0,1,2,6

Page 48: *The lynching of Henry Smith in Paris, Texas*

https://www.bing.com/images/search?view=detailV2&ccid=
Mlv7XJHI&id=68C69F697509235DF940586AB196D672800D53EA
&thid=OIP.Mlv7XJHIasxBgp5SVe3eJgHaFS&mediaurl=https%3a%2
f%2fc1.staticflickr.com%2f3%2f2346%2f2264601297_689db7386
8_z.jpg%3fzz%3d1&exph=357&expw=500&q=Lynching+in+paris%
2c+texas&simid=608023864159897515&selectedIndex=1&cbir=s
bi&ajaxhist=0

Page 58: *The Birdland Jazz Club back in the day*

https://commons.wikimedia.org/wiki/File:Birdlandclubentran
ce.jpg#/media/File:Birdland_club_entrance.jpg

Page 64: *Common sign of the times*

https://www.bing.com/images/search?view=detailV2&ccid=b
egzvMor&id=4247CF1BF03F1C7538995A9030B27AA1A5091AE1&
thid=OIP.RmsXgwJtzC3O-4jVhbjwHaDD&mediaurl=http%3a%2f%
2f1.bp.blogspot.com%2f-nNiq1C94a9k%2fTuylUq24JtI%2fAAAAA
AAAVJs%2fJTQc3ooD08s%2fs1600%2fwhites%2bonly.gif&exph=1
79&expw=434&q=WHITES+ONLY+SIGNS&simid=6080443854913
57082&selectedIndex=4&qft=+filterui%3alicenseType-Any&cbi
r=sbi&ajaxhist=0

Page 70: *Where's OSHA when you need them?*

https://www.bing.com/images/search?view=detailV2&ccid=6
bm8vy6Y&id=FD2994DAA52965C8A8E7B89B256466D08FB8A0DF
&thid=OIP.6bm8vy6YSyfdWPMusLBEdwHaC5&mediaurl=https%3
a%2f%2fwww.cuv3.com%2fwp-content%2fuploads%2fhine-featu
red.jpg&exph=250&expw=640&q=Hi-Rise+Metal+Workers&sImId
=608032033173540200&selectedIndex=25&qft=+filterui%3alicen
seType-Any&ajaxhist=0

Made in the USA
Columbia, SC
10 February 2019